SOPHIA BOOKS
'BRINGING SPIRIT INTO LIFE'

*A series of books which bring modern
spiritual ideas into life—for
practical use in everyday life.*

IN THE SAME SERIES:
The Journey Continues. . . Finding a New Relationship to Death
Dr Gilbert Childs with Sylvia Childs

Homemaking as a Social Art

Homemaking
as a Social Art

Creating a Home for
Body, Soul and Spirit

Veronika van Duin

SOPHIA BOOKS
Rudolf Steiner Press
London

Sophia Books
51 Queen Caroline Street
London W6 9QL

www.rudolfsteinerpress.com

Published by Sophia Books 2000
An imprint of Rudolf Steiner Press

A catalogue record for this book is available from
the British Library

ISBN 1 85584 068 5

Cover by Andrew Morgan Design
Typeset by DP Photosetting, Aylesbury, Bucks
Printed and bound in Great Britain by
Cromwell Press Limited, Trowbridge, Wiltshire

Contents

Acknowledgements

Very grateful thanks go to Siobhán Porter, Janet Coggin, Christine Lammers and Ann Druitt, who read, criticized and endlessly corrected my spelling and grammar! I couldn't have done this book without them.

Thanks also to Miriam Müller, Phil Flett and Helen O'Meara for their cheerful encouragement.

My most grateful thanks and love to my husband, Rob, who never gave up on me.

Author's Note

When I first started homemaking, it was for the sake of my daughter. I wanted her to experience as warm and happy a home as I had had. The principles that underpinned my very satisfactory childhood came from the remarkable work of Rudolf Steiner.

As a parent and homemaker with a growing family, I began to study his writing, wanting to understand what had fired my parents' ethics. From the study of spiritual science, practising what I had learned seemed a sensible next step. Then followed the request to pass it on to other homemakers, through workshops, lectures and seminars. The fruits are to be found in the pages of this book.

For the sake of flow and continuity, I have refrained from attributing specific principles on human development to Rudolf Steiner, but instead have included a bibliography from which source material homemakers wishing to do their own research can find a beginning. With these few words I wish to acknowledge my overwhelming debt to Rudolf Steiner's spiritual inspirations and very practical guidance for daily living.

Veronika van Duin

1.

Why Be A Homemaker?

The Role of the Home

In the world of today, the place of the home and its relevance to life in general has become something of an issue. We used to be quite content to assume a good home to be everyone's background, unless of course, they were underprivileged, impoverished, or of the criminal classes! Nowadays this assumption would not only be politically incorrect, but also factually at fault. A good home is not something everyone has. A place to sleep, to eat, and to receive some shelter seems to be all that many adults seek. And yet the need to return to family values, to a secure and solid home is heard as a *cri de coeur* from sociologists, psychologists and social workers.

As a result, not only sociological, but also educational and medical studies have been carried out, strongly suggesting that many human frailties, diseases and problems can be laid at the door of an empty and soulless home. It is becoming apparent that those people whose background is a harmonious, creative, empowering home are better adjusted to life and generally make good use of their intelligence. Those who suffer maladjustment, anti-social behaviour or are slow learners are often discovered to have had problems in their home, especially during childhood. A sound, healthy home is a foundation for a sound, healthy life.

People used to *live* at home, sharing hopes and aspirations, gaining fresh courage to face life's vicissitudes. In times gone by, children knew that when they were at home, Mother would be there and Father would come home to administer the expected discipline. There was a predictability about home. One knew where one was.

The woman's role was a fixed one. She represented the nurturing aspect in life; she cooked, cleaned, nursed, sewed, decorated, comforted, encouraged, listened and put her own needs second to everyone else's. She did not complain, at least not loudly. She accepted her lot as Eve's and bore her children in pain. The man's role was equally clear. His career was all-important, he was the hunter-father, the chastiser, the disciplinarian, the one-who-knows, the authority. He provided security, physical comforts, food, fire and maintenance.

In times much further in the past, the role of the woman in the home was different. She was the priestess-mother, the one who, in the home, ruled with an iron rod. Father took second place, waiting upon the priestess, offering his skills as hunter and protector. We lived in tribes, the nuclear family being quite unimaginable. Home was the warmth of the tribal hearth, shared by all who belonged. The nest-building instinct was an integral part of human develop-ment. However far back we go in history, the roles of woman and man were always clearly defined, though who had the power varied in different cultures and different parts of the world. As it still does today.

More recently, especially in our western society, the place of the woman began to feel restricted within society's narrow perception. It no longer seemed to suit the devel-oping consciousness and was becoming a role without a future. There were designated things she was permitted to do but so many more were denied to her. There was no equality, and freedom had to be sought within a given framework. Men, too, suffered from taboos and restrictions, but they were able to circumvent them because they held the power of decision politically, culturally and identifiably within society. With the work of the suffragettes the scales were tipped. We all know of the long hard haul womanhood has suffered to create a freer and more balanced role within society. Unfortunately this did not happen without casualties, the main ones being motherhood and home-making.

Because creating the home was seen as an essentially feminine task, with the rise of women's rights, feminism, and equality for all regardless of sex, the first place to take a beating was the home. All of a sudden (and certainly within the stream of history it occurred suddenly) it appeared that women refused to stay at home. Home lost its appeal as a place of refuge, as a nest, as a nurturing haven, and turned overnight into a trap, a pit, a prison where all hopes for fulfilment could never be realized.

Now that women are free to decide their role in life, as also are men, everyone wants to *get out there, into the real world, and get on in life.* One must suppose that home is not, then, a part of life or of the real world at all! And yet, there is a universal longing for a home, a safe place to be, where comfort, warmth and peace can be found. We dream of this lovely place, sometimes we create it, particularly for children as they seem to demand it more than adults or adolescents do. Old people also long for a home, but often have to settle for a bed-sit, granny-flat, or nursing home.

In our society today, home need not be a trap, a prison, an end to all development. Because we are becoming free human beings we can have a voice in the future. However, we need to get our priorities right. In these days of equality it can also be a man who stays at home. Does it matter who makes the home? But if a woman should choose to be a mother, carer or homemaker, is not this within her rights?

It is quite common to hear people say: 'I'm only a housewife. No, I don't work, I stay at home.' Whoever has stayed at home will know very well that this work is just as demanding as holding down a job. Nowadays there are many brave souls who do both; they have a career and take care of the home. If one comes home tired and still has to do all the household chores, is it any wonder that one gets resentful, angry and depressed? Did the happy home vanish with equal rights? It could be that in our eagerness to reach equality, we threw the baby out with the bath water. Men and women are equally good in the field of commerce, and men and women can be equally good at homemaking. The trick is to *share*. But before one can begin this community-building attempt, one must first recognize the necessity for a home and the foundation that it builds towards a sound social conscience. The modern homemaker is someone who has seen this amazing possibility and sets out to create an environment in which it can find its fulfilment.

The Modern Homemaker

Homemaking is a social art. Just as all artists practise their art, find new inspirations and explore their chosen field, so too does the homemaker need to learn about the social art, explore its possibilities and develop its potential. The foundation for the practice of the social art of homemaking lies in understanding the human being, not only with regard to physical necessities, but also in connection with psychological and spiritual needs, as well as expressions and qualities that live in everyone. Learning to live creatively with other people means learning about all our wonders, weaknesses and glorious potential. But it also means learning to recognize our dependence and influence on the totality of the world around us.

   If one studies humanity objectively, one will discover that every part of the human being can also be found in the world outside. Take for example the totality of the physical form, hair, skin, metabolic system, bones, blood, etc. The earth as an organism contains all these elements too. The plant world, the earth's crust, the rotting and absorbing of vegetation that enriches the soil, the stones, the rivers, etc. Or observe how the human being is dependent upon air in order to live. So too is the earth for any life to exist. The human being requires warmth and moisture. The earth has its sun and rain. One can go into finer detail and always arrive at the mutual reflection of humanity and the cosmos. The individual human being is a microcosm of the universe, which is the macrocosm.

This eternal harmonious principle will continue to work as long as humanity exists upon the earth. But human beings need to live within the macrocosm as true reflections, or else they destroy the environment upon which they are utterly dependent. We cannot live without the earth, its air, its water and warmth from the sun.

This state of being implies coexistence by means of reciprocal organisms. Such reciprocity also exists within society. For example, in an office that is part of a large business, the totality is mirrored on a smaller scale. The home too is a microcosm of outer social structures, being the smallest society that human beings have created. Because of this factor, what happens at home reflects in society at large and vice versa. Thus homes differ in different parts of the world and within different cultures, just as offices differ depending on the areas their business targets.

Nevertheless, every organization has its own focus and its own decision-making body, which is very often a single individual working within a corporate structure. The managing of a home is much the same, but with the powerful addition of the fact that what the home creates can make a fundamental difference to the future of society. The homemaker's task is a spiritual one, and can make a difference to human social development. Just as individual human beings can change the world, even altering the ecology of their environment, so too can a change in emphasis of the home life alter society. To do so, however, it requires a decisive step towards change and this means individual involvement and commitment.

Every human being has a distinctive identity, and so,

although we would like to be equal in rights, we do not all want to be the same and we value our identity, our uniqueness as individuals. To retain the self within its own personality it is necessary to have a head, heart and hands. The head *collects* the necessary facts, the heart *relates* to them and the hands *carry out* whatever decision has been reached.

The home too, needs a head, heart and hands. It needs its own *identity* towards which everyone who lives in it can orientate in order for decisions to be taken, and life to make progress. It requires a *homemaker* to lend it credibility as a viable organism. And as *synthesizer of the homelife* it is necessary for the homemaker to understand how everything can work at its best. We used to operate on instinct but the modern homemaker has the right to expect knowledge to become the basis of what we do, especially in relation to our daily life.

The Spiritual Value in Homemaking

We can no more expect an improvement in the ills of society without learning where we went wrong, than we can expect change in the lack of individual social abilities without learning about the social art. Every artistic expression finds its source in inspiration, which is a gift from the spirit. Homemaking is an artistic endeavour and so it too owes its source to ideals and aspirations. The ideals are to enhance health and vitality for every one in the home. The aspirations are to create an environment in which a new kind of social interaction based on freedom can come about. To start trying to make a difference in the world we need to know as much as we can about humanity and the world and their relationship to each other.

When we can see that the earth is a living organism, as is society, as is the home, as is the human being, then it follows that processes for creating life need to be present in each of these organisms. We find them as the basis of life for the earth in so far as it is a living being. If one observes with care, these living functions also manifest in the human being as seven processes fundamental to life. They are interconnected, yet individual and all seven need to function all the time. If one of them is absent, the living organism dies. If one or another is damaged or weak, then illnesses and complicated psychological conditions arise. They are as follows: *breathing, warming, nourishing, secreting, maintaining, growing,* and *reproducing*.

To understand them each as a separate process, as well as their dependency one upon the other, a new born baby can give us the clue. At birth the first sign of life is that the infant *breathes rhythmically* and immediately *contact and warmth* is established between parents and infant. Next the baby needs *nourishing*. Saliva is *secreted*, as are the digestive juices. The milk is absorbed, thus *maintaining* the infant's life and it begins the process of *growing*. For the next few years it *reproduces* what is learnt and gathered from daily life on earth until it can even reproduce its own kind. These are the seven life processes within the human being, but they can be understood in a far wider context as will be shown in the following chapters.

Within society, these processes are also present and they manifest as social states. The homemaker needs to understand these processes of life, both as human functions and as processes at work within the society of the home. These are the necessary colours, the substances, paintbrushes, and influences that form the social art of homemaking and they are expressed in the following way: *being active and resting; relating to each other; artistic and cultural interaction; answering needs; caretaking; self-development; consideration for each other.*

Like the life processes in the human being they each depend on the other. Each must be nurtured and cultivated, because they are all necessary when creating a living home. By examining them more closely as lively and healthy attitudes, the connection to the human life processes will become clear, as will the connection to the greater life processes at work in the universe. A brief outline of each of the living processes at work in the home serves as a prologue, setting the scene for an in-depth understanding to be developed in the following pages.

Living Processes within the Home

In every living organism, *activity and rest* are both present but unless they are harmonized in a rhythmic way, the home can be so busy that no rest can be found, or so laid back that no new inspiration can be resourced. The connection to the process of breathing becomes clear when we understand that just as breathing in a steady rhythm is vital for a healthy life, a steady pace of action alternating with peace and quiet is equally vital for a healthy life style.

Relating to each other and the world around requires interest and enthusiasm. We usually want to *like* other people! Warming to each other without becoming too passionately involved is the basis of I-You relationships. Society depends upon the capability of controlling attraction and rejection, just as human beings depend upon regulating body temperature in order to keep alive and well, the latter being the function of the life process of warming.

Colour, light, form and beauty as well as conversation create a stimulating, *cultured* and attractive home, satisfying the whole human being. Thus we can understand that nourishing the body is only one part of homemaking, (important, but not everything,) because the soul and spirit also hunger. An *artistic environment* offers nourishment to all aspects of the human being.

Answering needs appropriately is a secret to be discovered. Just as the human body knows exactly what chemicals to secrete in order to digest our food and deal with alien substances, which it subsequently excretes, so too in the home, balance and flexibility are keys to a comparably delicate and mysterious process. Too much or too little attention to needs creates either unhappiness or chaos in the home.

Caring for and maintaining the fabric of the home should include everyone, especially the homemaker. Because losing one's identity does not maintain sanity, as homemaker one should take good care of oneself! Here again, understanding how the process of maintaining works in the human body, compares remarkably to caretaking in the home. Including the homemaker in the upkeep of a bright and cheerful home becomes a matter of common sense and creates a vibrant quality of life.

Self-development is the right of every human being; thus individual and group development can create an exciting dynamic within the home. We may cease to grow in height, but will usually continue growing in life experience. The home can become a space in which the searching and creative mind can grow and change. Bearing in mind the inclusion of the homemaker in this space, homemaking can become an intellectual, as well as a practical challenge.

Co-operating with and *considering* other people, recognizing individual potential and being recognized in return, make the home a place where individual destiny can unfold. Taking up the task of homemaking puts one in the remarkable position of nurturing the purely human capacity to create. This is as much a part of the process of reproducing as is the bearing of children, because every birth of an idea, invention, skill or achievement carries the promise of a better life.

The seven living processes have some areas in common, which demonstrates their extraordinary interrelationship. Though each has its own strong identity and function, three aspects appear in all of them. *Conversation, food* and *sleep* connect them to each other. This is not difficult to comprehend because these three functions are essential to life itself. Without conversation, humanity would be unable to interact or make any social contact. Without food, whether it be for body, soul or spirit, humanity would die. Without sleep, which makes it possible to reach into a world richly endowed with meaning, humanity would wither. Because each living process has its own special way of bringing these essentials into a healthy relationship to daily life, they will naturally recur in the course of the following pages, but each time from a different standpoint. Learning about the creating of a home in which living qualities can flourish is a stimulating, challenging and worthwhile artistic endeavour.

The Purpose of Homemaking

If the home is to become a creative space that is both enjoyable and comfortable to live in, it would be better not to go back in time to stereotyped roles. Nor would we wish to, since so much energy has gone into finding freedom for the human being, regardless of sex. We usually aim to share the activities in the home between women and men. Nevertheless, the home can be described as being a place rather more feminine than masculine within our hearts and minds. There is a valid reason for this experience and it is not for nothing that it is more often the woman than the man who chooses to work at home.

Until recently in human development, women tended to approach life with a more holistic way of thinking, allowing feeling to play a large part in their destiny. Men, on the other hand, were generally more directional in their approach to life. We are, even today in this modern world of equality, not the same sex, neither in build, nor in inclination! But we can co-operate, co-create and co-work in the building of a new kind of home. Learning to appreciate our differences is the key to developing the aspects of thinking that we want to cultivate. Our freedom lies in the possibility of choice, rather than in our refusal to participate in such an important aspect of life. The social home can become a foundation of a new society that works towards recognition of, and respect for every human being.

When we choose to work as artists bringing fresh and vivid colour and form into the home, then we are creating a new kind of community. There are no blueprints for creating the perfect homemaker, neither does this book lay claim to any! There are, however, principles, aspects, attitudes and observations that a study of the seven life processes raises to consciousness. Once we decide to take them on board as part of our daily life, they will create the possibility of enjoying and developing homemaking as an expression of the social art and can bring social renewal a step nearer to fulfilment.

2.

Rhythm

Breathing

Breathing is the first thing we do at birth as soon as we have arrived in the world through the narrow birth-canal. This is our first independent activity. The little body expands into space and thereby draws air into itself for the first time. The surprise and pain of this experience compels the body to contract and the air is expelled into the world again. From then on expansion and contraction create a rhythm within the breathing system until that moment of life when the soul expands itself for the last time, contracts the lungs and expels the last breath on a great sigh. Throughout life, from that very first in-breath of birth until the last great out-breath of death, the human being breathes. This rhythmical exchange of air from the cosmos provides the foundation for the quality of our consciousness, which is in intimate relationship with this rhythmic process of breathing. Without breathing properly we lose consciousness, which is demonstrated by the fact that hyperventilating causes faintness and loss of consciousness.

Very small babies have a much faster rhythm of breathing than children or adults, or old people. Moreover, the infant's breathing is not only more rapid, but also irregular. As the infant grows in age and experience in the first three years, the rhythm of breathing gradually settles into a harmonious expansion and contraction of the rhythmic system. With this steadying of the breathing, conscious knowledge of self and the world begins. By the time the child can say *I* to itself, the breathing will have settled. It is still faster than an adult, but has become rhythmic. Only once the breathing is properly established can thinking really begin. Before this, the infant is completely dependent upon others for its physical and social needs. After the breathing steadies and the identity has begun to show itself, then the ability for social interaction with other human beings begins. The child starts to look for playmates and the social side of life begins its gradual process of development.

Breathing is a *taking-in* and a *giving-out*. The air is taken in and it is returned, changed by the body's needs. This principle of exchange exists in many other areas. Infants learn by example. The parent does something and the infant repeats it. The parent applauds, the infant delightedly repeats it. Human development is dependent upon exchange. Children brought up in isolation do not imitate, and thus do not learn. So we see that learning, too, is based on exchange, on the rhythmic give and take of one to another. By a kind of *soul breathing* we take in the world, absorb and imitate what is around us, and then we return what we have gained by doing what was set before us as example. Hence, if little children behave badly, we have to look first to ourselves before chastising them. What was it they breathed in from our example? As the infant becomes older, this dependence on example lessens. But what has been laid down in those first three years remains as a solid foundation, for better or for worse.

Since from infancy we take in the world and return it by imitation, as long as our senses are all in working order we will perceive everything in the world around us quite indiscriminately. Choice only lies in what we are able to select and raise to conscious awareness. Small children have not yet acquired the ability to select or to ignore sense-impressions. They receive everything, just like breathing in the air. If overloaded with impressions they will react with hyperactive behaviour, being unable to shut down the activity of the senses. The child will tend to become over stimulated, nervous and fussy. With too few impressions the senses remain asleep, undernourished and inactive. The child may tend to lie inert, under-stimulated and under-developed. What is established in early childhood has its effect on health in later life.

Again it is rhythm that creates the harmony. Alternating stimulation, perception and activity with peace, sleep and silence enables the baby to grow in its powers of thinking as naturally and harmoniously as it should. Such things were cared for in the parenting traditions of times gone by. Babies were strapped to their mother's body for quite a long time so that they could sleep, feed and experience the world from within the warm embrace of the maternal body of life. After all, we begin our way into life on earth in the dark, warm wetness of the womb. Only then are we plunged into the light, air and activity of the world. This must be a great shock. It takes the next few years to recover, and to orientate in the alien, huge and cold world. These things need to be eased. As breathing takes time to settle, so too does rhythm in the senses need time to settle into perceptions that are sound and based on reality. Rhythm in a baby's life will set it on a path of healthy perception and the first step to learning can be sound and wholesome.

Rhythm can quite easily be established. It lives in the small things of daily life, such as the feeding rhythm, and the playing and sleeping rhythms. Here lies the possibility for songs to appear and then reappear, for gestures and activities to be learned and to be repeated. Rhythm lies in the familiar regularity of small daily events. Surprises, too, can be included in the rhythms that are established, since rhythm is not routine. Routine is repetitive, formed and certain. Rhythm is alive, creative, a breathing between events, actions and thoughts. Rhythm lies at the base of melody and harmony, and melody can have variations. Routine lies at the base of beat. Routine does indeed have its part to play but it is better placed in relation to the life processes of maintaining where the regularity of renewal is required. To create melody and harmony between expansion and contraction as we experience it unconsciously in breathing is the first necessity for a healthy life style.

A life style without rhythm also has its effect. We cannot function clearly when we cannot anticipate the next thing and everything arrives as a small shock, or brings disappointment with its absence. We become anxious and over react, or paralysed in the face of too many surprise happenings. This anxiety can become an unconscious foundation for illness. A sound rhythm of life will become the basis for a healthier body in the future. This is especially so for children suffering from illnesses of the lungs and skin, (both important for the body's breathing) such as asthma and eczema, or those with conditions such as autism, hyperactivity or hyperventilation.

By developing rhythms in life, which correspond to the needs of children, one may begin to harmonize any unsettled experiences of contraction and expansion. Working with the living rhythms in the world is the way to bring harmony into our daily life.

Rhythm in the Year

There are rhythms already present in the world which we, as human beings, reflect in various ways. As a fascinating start to becoming a social artist, the homemaker can discover these rhythms and begin to weave them into daily life.

There are the seasons of the year, more strongly marked in temperate zones, taking us through weather changes that can affect our mood. Perhaps a wet day makes us more sober, whereas sunny days can brighten us and encourage us to do all kinds of energetic things. Summer and winter have an effect too. For example, it is more difficult to concentrate our thoughts and to study in the heat of summer than it is in the cooler parts of the year. Some people love the summer. Their energy level rises, their ability to socialise and make friends is much higher in the light, warm days of the year. But in winter these people tend to become more introverted. There are some who even suffer from depression in the darker days and longer nights of winter. Autumn and spring move the scales of the year from the expansion of high summer to the contraction of deep winter. Many people find these seasons of transition the most unsettling, where the anticipation of the dark is a foreshadow of depression, or the coming light is a tantalizing prophet of joy and activity. Other people find these equinoctial seasons pleasant in that they are neither this nor that and within their balance the inner self can rest. In those countries where seasons hardly exist the rhythm of light and darkness is very striking. Balancing these strong impressions can be taken up within the home and reflected in the life style.

Children are more at the mercy of the fluctuating seasons than are adults, and it is the home that provides the necessary protection and stabilizing influence. To make this natural and easy so that a healthy relationship to nature can be formed, bringing a reflection of the seasons into the home is of benefit to all age groups because it can highlight the different ways in which we are dependent upon, and supported by, nature. Books such as *Family, Festivals and Food*, as well as *All Year Round* are full of excellent ideas for the homemaker who has small children. Taking note of festivals that human beings throughout the ages have created in relation to the seasons' changes is a wonderful way of harmonizing nature's rhythm with that of the human being. Within the home it gives rise to the opportunity to become artistic and creative.

Celebrating the seasonal festivals at home creates a fundamental rhythm. Christmas comes around every year, as do Hanukkah, Ramadan, Easter or the less religious festivals such as Mid-Summer or Hallowe'en. Festivals mark peak and trough moments in the year. We do not celebrate all the time, just as it is neither mid-winter, nor mid-summer all the year long! The rhythm of festivity and lull, celebration and daily chores, makes the year swing round effortlessly and interestingly. The preparation towards a festive time means that everyone is involved. Certainly children love these times, making decorations and baking biscuits. Though adolescents often profess disinterest in festivals, they will more often than not secretly enjoy the bustle and will generally participate if it is an open invitation. Creating a festive mood brings people together. And if the festival is marked not only for its outer value, but also for its inner aspects, its deeper purpose, then it refreshes us and revives potential. Family traditions are precious and they make the ground of our lives safe.

To become a homemaker means to utilize whatever the world can offer as a basis for developing the social art. The world offers its seasons and if homemakers make good use of these rhythms a renewed relationship to time will come about. To be *in time* is a lovely expression. It means to live in the present, to be *here and now*. Unimaginatively we use it only to equate with punctuality. Maybe if we relearned the value of the experience of time as the cycle of the year, we would once again be literally *in time*. Where children are concerned, this is essential. They live in the present, and to them time is only relative. The concept of time as moments on a direct path of success is unreal. They understand that time is a soul quality, not a physical commodity. This is why it is so difficult to make children hurry. By rushing them, we make them fractious, nervous and irritable. The hyperactive child especially will benefit from a strong steady rhythm in the year. People with special needs will recognize the cycle of the year and orientate themselves better in a world that is so often hard to understand.

To live according to the cycle of the seasonal and festive year is fun, creative and wholesome. All of us can find reassurance and security in the certainty of the rhythm of the seasons and their relevant celebration. The homemaker, by setting out the purpose of a particular festival, can endow daily work with new meaning by involving everyone in the preparation. Even if the home is made up of adults only, one can change a picture on the wall and mark the season with appropriate food and flowers. It will lift up the mood and create a peak of difference in the year.

Rhythm of the Week

The home becomes an interesting place to be when each day takes on real purpose. Every day is different. For a start, we may wake up in a different mood on different days because each day carries its particular challenge. For those who are out of work and have nothing to do, each day takes on a sameness, and boredom can lead to a feeling of hopelessness. We may sometimes resent the daily chores, but their purposeful character is, in fact, a lifeline to *meaning*. Without meaning we can lose *hope*.

Part of the art of homemaking is to highlight rhythm, and the most important rhythm is the seven days in the week. This is the fundamental rhythm of ordinary life and it is linked to a very spiritual rhythm by its connection to the seven moving planets. The number seven is always connected to living processes. There are seven basic notes to our musical scale. Even our life on earth can be seen as marked out in a rhythm of seven-year periods, each bringing its own developmental changes, as we shall see in the concluding chapter.

The ancients recognized that certain activities belong to certain days, since they ascribed each day to a planet. They recognized certain attributes related to each planet and gave it personality. In those days, the Earth was seen to be the fixed centre of the universe, the Sun being one of its planets, and in the following context therefore, it remains a planet. The Sun belonged to the *god of light*, the Moon to the *god of form*, Mars to the *god of war*, Mercury to the *messenger god*, Jupiter to the *god of wisdom*, Venus to the *god of love*, and Saturn to the *god of judgement*. We still retain these names in the days of the week. Sunday is an obvious example since it contains the name of the planet to which it is connected. Monday too, retains the name of the Moon. Tuesday is less clear because it comes from the Germanic language, but in French we have *Mardi* which clearly links us to Mars. Wednesday connects us to Wodin, which is the Norse for Mercury. Thursday also derives from the Norse god, Thor, who translates as Jupiter for the Romans. Friday, Freya's day, is the Norse for Venus, and Saturday returns us to the Latin, in Saturn. Thus each day has its own special character. At home one can create for each day a particular mood, not outwardly, but by bringing towards it an inner attitude appropriate to the day's special quality.

The week-days are busy, active outgoing days. The week-ends are inner soul-developing days. Once again we experience expansion and contraction at work in the rhythm of the week. This is not something new. We have always maintained the need for a rest-day in the week. The question is how we use it. Is it a rest? Or is it filled up with all the chores we could not get through during the week because we were too busy to do them?

It is very easy to use every waking moment at home to catch up on what has not yet been covered! For some people who work at home, this can become an unconscious habit. Then days that could be highlighted with cultural or leisure activities might become too few or too far between. For those who work outside the home, the week-ends may be the only time in which to do everything. By relegating certain chores to certain days a rhythm can begin to work in which appropriate rest-days can have their place as an important element within the framework of the week. Rhythm is an essential ingredient to bring about order in daily life.

Rhythm of the Day

For rhythm to exist and not wholly fall into routine, some understanding of what lies behind it must be cultivated. We have already explored the fact that rhythm relates to breathing. It also relates to the activity of our senses. We take in sense impressions in a rhythm of contraction (i.e. taking in impressions), and expansion (i.e. giving back knowledge of the world), for example, when we talk and listen. Whilst speaking we use our senses to express ourselves, becoming sometimes very active indeed! Whilst listening, we have to settle down inwardly and become silent and still in order to absorb and comprehend what we are hearing and seeing. We do this rhythmically in every experience of all our senses. What we perceive, for example through seeing, which means becoming actively engaged with what is visible, gives us a knowledge about the world around us, which means absorbing quietly what we have learnt. Breathing and the human ability of perception are directly linked. Since our senses are active all the time, rhythm in the day must be sought, in order to create a harmony so that conscious knowledge can be used and not burnt up, or passively absorbed.

There are some very natural rhythms. We work hard, or we play hard, and then we are tired so we rest. From this peaceful experience we continue our activity refreshed and with renewed energy. Since the world today moves very much faster than in the past, it has become necessary to speed up our own natural rhythm to keep pace. Then, when moments arise in which we can unwind, it can often mean that we do not make good use of them! If this happens, we can even feel bored, not realizing that this is, in fact, because we are tired.

There is a legitimate time in one's life when this state of mind is most prevalent and this is during the phase of adolescence. It can be helpful to remember this feeling when such moments occur in one's adult life. However, after adolescence being bored often means that one has not been stretched enough in a creative way. One may have been rushing around being busy, or being over-stimulated by too much physical speed. Or one may have been sitting too long, becoming tired from using the intellectual aspects of thinking. Boredom in adolescence may signify that one is finding one's own relationships to strengths and weaknesses. But in children or adults it can be a sign that there is a lack of rhythm in daily life.

The perfect balance between work, rest, study, and entertainment, sleep and wakefulness is not a recipe that anyone can give. It depends on the individual, since there can be no perfect rhythm that suits everyone. Sometimes we fall back on routine to level out individual needs of rhythm in life because to create a separate rhythm for each person in the house would drive the homemaker to distraction. Clearly, a compromise must be reached.

We need to find a rhythm in which we can all share, a rhythm that still leaves the individual free to come and go within it, by paying attention to certain key moments of the day. They are the *morning* and *evening* hours, *meal times,* and the alternation of *work and play* versus *periods of rest.*

We all go to sleep and wake up. We each have our own particular way of doing this, but usually we sleep at night and are awake during the day. Those mornings when there is enough time to get organized peacefully usually lead to a good day. Those evenings when we are given the space and time to unwind, relax and centre ourselves in relation to all we have experienced during the day usually lead to a good night's sleep.

If during the day we balance our activity with tea-breaks, don't we feel a great deal more able to cope with stresses? Educational establishments and places of employment make regular breaks in the day. It is known to improve performance. It is also recognized that too many, or too long a break, can create loss of energy and motivation. Homemakers too, require breaks, for if they work and only work all day, then an exhausted, resentful person greets the home-comers, often with a demand to contribute towards the household chores.

Homemakers are in the happy position of being able to create a rhythm to suit themselves. Though babies and small children may be at home with all the attendant needs, the homemaker, by creating a rhythm relating to these requirements, can experience a certain sense of freedom within the home, whereas those who enter employment may find more restrictions set upon them by agencies other than their own initiative. The needs of the home and the personal needs of the homemaker can be worked out amicably. An employee does not often have this freedom.

Another rhythm in the day that deserves a great deal of credit is the regularity of meal times. It suits the digestive system. It also suits all the senses. Since they are dependent upon the body's smooth functioning, to eat at regular times in the day is a good rhythm, but more importantly, to take a moment of silence before eating for an in-drawing of breath, and to do the same at the end of the meal, is not just a thought-out religious rite. It is an aid to absorbing not only the food, but also each other. The rhythm of meal times offers precious moments when the house-community meets, and then separates again.

Eating is a social grace and can be graced as a social gift. On special social occasions, such as parties, food is usually included in the celebration. People sit down, breathe in, take note of each other, and share around a meal. Children who grow up with family meals appearing rhythmically throughout the day are more able to become socially capable and interesting adults. Meal times are moments of learning something about each other. And this requires a moment of respect before and after, for the food that we eat and the companions we are graced to have. In homes where there are no children, or where groups of people choose to live together, the rhythm of the meal may be the only time of meeting each other.

Perhaps some of the stress-related disorders that appear in young children, as well as problems with social interaction with their peers and with adults may be connected to irregular or solitary meals. The breakfast-bar cannot quite replace the dining table, and TV dinners are rather lonely affairs. Unfortunately, in our very active life of today, we seem to have lost some of our instinct for rhythm in relation to early childhood and this can bring difficulties later for both parents and offspring as they learn how to live toge-ther. It can mean that individual rhythms find too few moments of reconciliation, and this is inclined to lead to social conflict within the home.

It is possible to assist the founding of an easy and relaxed way of relating to life's ups and downs by attending to the rhythms of early childhood. Rhythm is created very early on in infancy. The baby cries and usually the parent immediately reacts. If, by gradual and gentle persuasion, the individual rhythm of the infant can be adjusted by the parent, regularity follows. Once this is established and adhered to, then every member of the family can know when there will be peace and when activity is necessary.

Lastly, a moment for oneself should be built into each day. Finding a rhythm between human contact and moments alone is essential for sanity and inner balance. But again, the rhythm will be an individual one. Each of us must find out what the best rhythm is. Some need more solitude, some need less. Human beings are individuals, who experience life, health and activity, each in their own particular way. Nevertheless, although we each have our own constitution, we share the fact of being physical, experiencing emotions, and expressing our individuality.

A renewed understanding of the human being can help towards establishing a home in which children, adolescents and adults can be mutually interactive in a beneficial way. To do this we need to understand that the human being consists of *various* states, or bodies, each of them having different tasks within the whole. The fourfold division is perhaps the most relevant in the context of rhythm in life, because it explains how the human being is made of body, life, soul and identity, all of which should work together in harmony.

The Fourfold Human Being

When a child is first conceived it is not uncommon for either parent, or both, to feel that they already know their child. Often it is the mother who experiences this most strongly. Then, when the baby is born, it can be as if a familiar little person has arrived in the family. And yet this infant is tiny and weak, needing a great deal of care.

This experience of individuality, even before the child is born, does not always fit the physical reality at birth. It takes time for the two to harmonize, sometimes right into adulthood. As the infant grows from babyhood to child-hood and adolescence and into maturity, life experience is gathered. Everyone reacts differently to events in life. Emotions are not expressed identically in human beings.

We are all very different and experience ourselves to be unique. The individuality which expresses itself over and above any physical or emotional demonstration can be called the *ego*—the spirit of the human being. This *spirit*, the ego, is eternal and so can be perceived even at conception, or before. The ego leads the individual throughout life, and is the spirit that the homemaker is called upon to acknowledge in each individual, whatever their specific needs, thoughts and attitudes. Without a recognition of the uniqueness of the individual the home could become merely an institution.

The *body* is the *physical* aspect of the human being. It is made up of earthly matter and chemical substances that can be found everywhere in the world, and which, after death, return to the world. The physical body is therefore most susceptible to earthly influences. It requires great care and attention. Neglecting the physical body leads to illness. Homemakers are almost entirely caught up in caring for and satisfying the needs of this aspect of humanity.

How can the physical body hold together in life, and then dissolve into the world after death? What is it that makes it alive and gives it form? It is the principle of the *life body* or the *ether body*. Everything living has some ether substance around it. It is not visible, or tangible when active, except perhaps as an inner experience of light, which can be felt when in the presence of small babies, or very old people at the edge of life. It can be understood by its absence, because then life dies and what is physical disintegrates and returns to its chemical origins. Because of the ether, or life body, we can retain form in our physical structure so that what is eternal—the ego—can live in the world as a human being.

What brings these three into a coherent and creative connection with each other is the *soul*, or *astral body*. The soul includes that part of the human being that makes relationships, and which, amongst other things, mediates between the inner feelings and emotions of the individual, and emotions, actions and statements coming from outside.

Because the individual ego connects to the astral body, it can control our impulsive actions and desires and humanize our motives and instincts. Thus we are not, as are the animals, driven to actions but can exercise decision and choice. And we are, moreover, unlike the animals that belong to a species, physically unique in our outer form.

To sum up, one can say: the *ego* is the spirit or unique individuality. The *astral* body embraces the soul that is the bearer of emotions, feelings and instincts. The *ether* body is the life body of forces that give life and form to matter. And the *physical* body comprises material or chemical substances belonging to the earth.

Homemakers need to work closely with these aspects, encouraging health in all four areas. To create an environment where life experience can nourish the astral body and ego, where rhythm can offer health to the physical body by allowing its life forces or ether body to work harmoniously, is a very sound reason for protecting the home.

Our present society offers great stimulation, but also challenges, which may at times have the tendency to drain us of our strength and energy. Coming home means to be where the four bodies or states of being are appropriately addressed, and can renew themselves. Recognizing the rhythm created by day and night can help us to bring about a restorative quality to life, which enables our feelings and power of thought to function more harmoniously. When we are in harmony with our inner selves, our consciousness is greatly enhanced, but it also works within its own life-sustaining rhythms.

Rhythm in Consciousness

Understanding the human being is part of the task of homemaking, and this can be accomplished by recognizing certain needs in daily life that provide the means to enhance our spiritual development. The fundamental rhythm of life is that of sleeping and waking. The need to sleep as well as to be awake is as important as the need to breathe in and breathe out. Homemakers need to be in touch with these

contrasting aspects of consciousness in order to harmonize
them creatively.

During the day we are able to think clearly and precisely.
But what of that other state, the state of sleep, in which we
spend quite a lot of time? How is it that we can take up
today where we left off last night? Where do we go when
we sleep? We know quite well that we are not non-existent
during sleep, we are only unconscious. Science informs us
that the unconscious contains more knowledge than we
make use of in daily life. We are told, when we suffer
psychological problems, that the answer can be raised up out
of our sub-conscious. Thus we can conclude that we have a
night-consciousness as well as a day-consciousness. Clearly
they are not the same. They are, however, interdependent.

We place a great deal of store by our day-consciousness.
This is the state of mind that we believe is the most
effective. After all, we seem to get nothing done during
sleep! But if we go back in time to ancient history, we find
that those who were the leaders of humanity expected to
get more done whilst they were unconscious to the world.
Human beings remembered their experiences during sleep
as spending time with their angels, or gods, who gave of
their wisdom. For instance, the Angel Gabriel appeared to
Mary in a dream. In Greek mythology, Zeus, the god of
wisdom, appeared to Leda in the guise of a swan in order to
lie with her. The sibyls of ancient Greece entered into
trances in which wisdom was shown to them by the gods of
nature such as Pan, with his cloven hoofs and horns of a
goat, playing his pipes of enchantment. In every mythology, wisdom was given to human beings via the unconscious, or during sleep. Today, though our waking
consciousness does not always believe such things, we still
often do have moments when a dream can become a guide
to the following day's events or actions.

There are many stages of consciousness between the
rhythm of day- and night-consciousness. We live in these

intermediate rhythms all the time. Both adults and children often daydream. It is the imagination at work. One can work all day on automatic pilot, cleaning, cooking and shopping, with one's mind elsewhere in a private world, or one can concentrate exclusively on an event or task, not aware of anything outside the sphere of focus. We are able to contract into ourselves and expand into another dimension. This is the place of imagination, intuition and inspiration. It is where we go when we seek to create, or seek refuge from the dull routine of ordinary life. It is here that homemakers can find restoration and new ideas.

Our day-consciousness can also expand into study, business, and work. These are the moments when we can be very efficient whilst the imagination goes to sleep. We alternate all the time, expansion in one sense being contraction in another. To our unconscious, wisdom-filled night-consciousness, being awake is a focus, a contraction. To our clear, waking day-consciousness, being asleep is a contraction. It is the rhythm between the two states which gives us knowledge of our inner selves and the world. Because of this alternating state of consciousness, we know ourselves to be not only matter, but also spirit. We know our thoughts are not material, though they can be translated into matter. For example, every modern convenience was once spirit when it was a pure thought.

Just as we can meet friends and family in our everyday state of consciousness, the spirit and soul can meet companions in the world that we enter when we sleep. These beings are known as angels, and spiritual tradition ascribes an angel to each human being on earth, which we call the guardian angel. In former times this was common knowledge and speaking to angels as well as seeing them in every living thing as the bringer of life and health was commonplace. The angel was known to inspire saints and to be a comforting companion in sorrows and trials. Artists painted angels frequently and beautifully in any scene connected to a spiritual event. Later, the angelic companion vanished from the canvas, but an aura of light was painted round the head of highly developed human beings. Nowadays, talking to angels lives on in children, who can still speak freely about it and can even describe them imaginatively. As we grow older we can no longer so easily converse consciously with spiritual beings and are inclined not to believe in the guardian angel. Scepticism can blur our inner sensitivity, and yet we know when in great need that someone watches over our destiny, and we can find a kind of inner peace when we allow there to be something greater than ourselves at work in the mysteries of our daily joys and sorrows. During sleep we are more able to reach these helpers and guides, and what happens when we do not sleep properly is that we are cut off from our guardian angel. Those who suffer from insomnia know how quickly life gets out of proportion. To be totally deprived of sleep is a slow cause of death, and this is because we cannot converse with our angels who give us life.

Our day-consciousness is vital. Equally, our night-consciousness is essential to restore us and bring balance into all perceptions, which flood our being. Sleep, or unconsciousness, is not an absence of self. It is the ability to reflect upon and retain the sense perceptions of daily life in the life sustaining mirror of the angel's gaze. Thus it is of particular importance for a healthy life of thought, feeling and activity that we sleep enough and soundly. The home that encourages its members to respect the restorative quality of sleep, as well as paying attention to precious moments of peace, becomes a powerful preventive against depression, stress and burn-out.

Rhythm of Sleeping and Waking

To be awake means that the previously mentioned four bodies connect with each other and relate to the world around. This state of consciousness is limited to what is physically possible. In contrast, sleep means to be aware of another world, a non-material, spiritual world that is not limited in this way. During sleep, the four bodies maintain a looser connection with each other. The ego and astral body, being closely related, remain in contact with each other but lift themselves away from the physical body, (which continues to breathe and live by virtue of the faithful ether body), and they converse with our spiritual companions. In sleep we expand our consciousness, and on waking contract into the every day world, bringing back all there is to know of the spirit world. Though we cannot always remember our heavenly conversations, this does not mean that they have not taken place!

There is a saying: *to sleep on a question or a problem.* Another proverb states: *the night brings its wise counsel.* How many times has this proved to be the case! Somehow one knows in the morning what to do about something which yesterday seemed insoluble or too awful to contemplate. Conversely, there are those sleepless nights when we have fought like Jacob, who wrestled with an angel, or grappled with our own private demons, unable to rest because of deeds done, or undone. Then the morning is not welcome as a bringer of wisdom. It is only welcome as a distraction.

The spiritual world is peopled not only with angels, but with ranks of angelic beings. We can read in books on occult matters, as well as in most religious writings, about angels, each having a role and purpose as servant of the creator-power, or godhead, different religions calling him by different names. These beings surround our earth and work within their given realm for the development of humanity.

It is with these beings that we converse when we sleep and this is why our unconscious is so wise. In conversation with them we know and see all that was and all that is to be. We retain only a fraction of what we know from this night-time experience in our waking life. Those who meditate or pray may retain a little more. Those who have not been pushed into early intellectual development, retain still more. To see a little baby sleep is to know it is still in heaven. To see an old person sleep is to know that the way home is open. It is in the life between these two ages that we need to pay more attention as to how we sleep and how we wake.

Going to Sleep

The positive, and nicest way to go to sleep is to prepare for it peacefully and happily. With children this is delightfully easy if no one is in a great hurry. Getting ready for bed is the ideal opportunity for conversation, for chatting, and listening to the day's adventures. One can make the bedroom nice, get the clothes ready for the morning, settle down to a good story, sing songs, recite poems, look at pictures, or just share some secrets. It is a time for intimacy. Candlelight creates a lovely atmosphere in which joys, sorrows and fears can be confided by the child. It is intimacy of the most precious kind and it forms the foundation for a lifetime's trust in each other.

In adolescence, going to sleep is often something to be avoided. To talk about contact with a guardian angel is not easily accepted nowadays, yet a good friend or parent will be acutely aware of how much anxiety there is about being alone and not in control of one's destiny. This is often the reason for not wanting to go to bed because in sleep we cannot decide who and what we will meet. So an opportunity for a late-night chat can allow a peaceful, healing space, from which the young person can go to bed feeling safe and sound. To be available for easing transition moments is a most precious part of homemaking.

However, in caring for others, homemakers should not forget their own needs. A good book, a relaxing conversation, settling down to reflect for a moment on the day's events, acknowledging successes and failures, these are all healthy unwinding processes. They allow a breathing space. They make it possible to let go, in a responsible way, of all the tensions that the responsibilities of daily life impose, because we take the results of the day into our sleep. In so doing, we are not at liberty to leave behind any unresolved unpleasantness, which we may have experienced or expressed. This too, accompanies us into the night. What was true and meaningful of conversations and deeds can be understood by the angelic beings. What was brittle and meaningless, such as electronic noises, which the radio and television emit, cannot be comprehended. To refrain from television or electronic music last thing before sleeping is helpful. The angels share in what is living. They follow with intense interest the thoughts, feelings and deeds of human beings.

For sleep to be healthy and bring good counsel in the morning, it is better to heal the quarrels and discords that may have arisen during the day, before going to bed. It is also helpful to ensure that children need not fall asleep with unexpressed miseries, however small they may seem. Those days that do not run as smoothly as one would wish, may be the result of knotted and difficult encounters of the day before, for which we could find no resolution in sleep. Never go to sleep on a quarrel, is good advice!

The angels, who can be our guides and helpers, can only draw near to us when our sleep is natural. Alcohol and sleeping pills do not really assist this process. They actually separate the astral body from the ego, an unnatural act, which is the reason why we lose consciousness, but this is not, in truth, real sleep. Perhaps a change in the rhythm of life, and an emphasis on sorting out, rather than blocking out problems, can bring a more refreshing slumber. Once a good sound sleep can be assured, it is a positive and healthy vantage point from which to manage one's daily life.

Waking-up

To awaken gently and in a cheerful way is such a lovely experience. Children generally look forward to the day because they have so many things that they are eager to experience. A friendly greeting, a helping hand, with time to get organized and time to eat, with time to get to school and play with friends before the lessons begin—all this makes a lovely day. All that is required is that the parent gets up in time to start this harmonious process! For a child to begin the day unprepared and possibly hungry is a recipe for irritation, nervousness and lack of concentration. Adults too, can create a bad day for themselves on the same premise. How one awakens so very often depends upon what the night contains.

Adolescents generally find it difficult to get up. Just as they cannot go to sleep, so too do they seem unable to rise until it is almost too late. This insecurity about life in general, owing to lack of experience, can make facing the day an almost insurmountable wall. Refraining from shouting, nagging and recriminating is the best way to ensure that the young person can have a productive and enjoyable day. If childhood had a well established rising time, this will return again once the teenager reaches adulthood.

Adults also need time to awaken. It is helpful to have a few minutes to survey the day, to get a feel of things to come. Time to dress and eat helps as well. If we are in a hurry, it is often because we try to snatch the longest possible time to sleep, and allow ourselves the shortest possible time to get ready for the day. Just as time is a necessity for children in the morning, it is equally necessary for adults, especially if we want to encourage confidence and security around us.

Many homemakers find themselves rushing around getting everyone organized and sitting down with a cup of coffee only after everyone has gone. Then they feel as though a whole day has already passed, and only at this point is there time to breathe! The homemaker who also goes out to work, cannot even afford this luxury. Thus it would be a good idea to have some peace *before* everyone gets going, rather than not at all.

To be able to think clearly and with imagination, we need to start from the strong position of inner relaxation. This can happen best if we sleep well and soundly so that we can move harmoniously between the two states of consciousness. However, the rhythm of day- and night-consciousness is utterly dependent upon *how* one goes to sleep and *how* one wakes up. It is, in fact, so linked that poor sleep can be the source of some of the stress that can lead to depression. If such conditions do happen, it would be helpful to take a look at these areas, because they may reveal why on some days alertness can progressively deteriorate.

It is easiest to start by taking care of the evenings. Then the morning will be good, the day will be kinder, and sleep will be sound. This is the most essential of all the rhythms that have been described. It may seem at times to be a small contribution on the part of the homemaker, but it is in fact the cornerstone of a balanced and healthy mentality.

Problems with Rhythm

The greatest hindrance to rhythm is society's addiction to speed. Everything has to be achieved yesterday as though we have no time any more! We also often pressurize ourselves and our children to succeed, placing great store on efficiency and intellect. As homemakers we may expect ourselves to care for the home and also have a career. In general, expectations are very high in our present society. One reason is financial. We need money to live, but perhaps we do not need to work like mad to have enough for our leisure and then have no time to enjoy it! It could be more wholesome to reinvest in the home as a valid place in which to work, to socialize and simply to live.

Modern society has a tendency to live for the future, always seeking to achieve. To do this one cannot rest, but must forever be on the move. Is the experience of the speeding up of time an expression of fear of meeting the future? Has it become necessary to rush towards it in order to control it, rather than walk steadily towards it whilst it is being created? We make our own future by how we relate to the present. Thus home could be a place in which to relax, to share and regenerate energy. But it depends upon taking time and living in the present.

Homemakers will recognize certain tendencies working against us in our wish to enjoy our work within the home. These may be feelings of heaviness, resentment, and lack of energy, or dissatisfaction, leading to the need to make excuses and hurry through the work in order to move on to something else. These negative feelings can happen to anyone in any walk of life. Often, when faced with recurring patterns in one's life, it helps to identify the underlying problem in order to deal with it creatively. On careful examination of the above social ailments, it shows that something, or someone, is behind the inertia and misery. In olden times, we might have called it the Devil, but nowadays we recognize that evil has many faces. Just as there are angels and ranks of angels assisting human progress, so are there dark beings upon beings that hinder human development. These uncomfortable influences from which we suffer are beings of great power. The most mighty of these negative spiritual forces, unlike the godhead or creator-being, can be experienced as twofold, their power of deception all the greater in their opposition to each other. For the sake of clarity, and so that we can overcome them with deliberate positivity, it is helpful to identify them by name.

The one can be called Ahriman, the dark god of the

ancient Persian mysteries. The Persians believed that the sun had the power to make all things grow and that the darkness inside the earth killed all life. So the story tells that the sun-god gave human beings a golden dagger, a plough, which cut into the dead earth and filled the furrows with light. With this the darkness of Ahriman was overcome and the seeds could come up into the light of the sun and be the first food grown by human beings.

The other we can describe as Lucifer, the fallen flaming angel, or the tempter in Paradise. The myth of the defeat of this high-ranking archangel of light, who sought to be like God and was cast down as a snake with its belly on the earth, is a story we can all understand. Though mythologies from different parts of the world identify these beings by other names, nevertheless, the darkness of evil and the temptations of bright demons exist in every true spiritual tradition.

Homemakers are not immune to these universal powers and host them as unwelcome house-guests who creep into our moods and thoughts. Ahriman colours our outlook with soulless efficiency, possessiveness, envy, and fear. Enjoyment of life does not exist on his list of priorities. Lucifer tempts us into self-gratification, ambition, unwholesome pride, and concern with appearances. Attitudes such as devotion, reverence, and wonder are too simple for his complex intentions.

All human beings face these challenging powers, and if handled with the strength gained by recognizing their might, the hindrances turn into a part of our development, because without them we could have no freedom. Development depends upon overcoming obstacles, but most of all, upon recognizing them in the first place. However, to help us we need to focus on reliable guides whom we may follow on a safe middle path between such obstacles. For example, we can learn from the Buddha who first showed humanity the way to overcome burdensome matter and high-flying ambition. He taught us the path of *compassion* for all living things. After him came Christ with his great message and example of *love*.

As homemakers we are drawn to follow such liberating aspirations because we recognize the chains with which Ahriman ties us up in resentment and depression and we recognize Lucifer's mockery in the misery of burning with unfulfilled desires and anxieties. By cultivating rhythm in the home, using outer activity tempered by inner peace, these subtle voices are stilled, and in this way we can learn to live in the present. Striving for compassion and love provides the necessary protection, and helps us to find the strength required to tread a balanced path.

Rhythm at Home

Rhythm in the home depends upon someone beginning the melody played out by activity and rest. Then others will take it up in their own special way and harmony will sound, just as each instrument in an orchestra adds its own special tonal quality to the symphony being played. The home-maker is like the conductor of an orchestra. The music will only be as good, clear and light as is the guidance coming from the conductor. But there would be no use in con-ducting if the musicians could not play their instruments, or did not know how to keep in rhythm with each other! Just as music relies on rhythm for its meaning and harmony, so does the home rely on in- and out-breathing of action and peace in order for harmony to be maintained.

As soon as homemakers recognize that homemaking is an art to be rediscovered, the members of the house-community, whatever their age, become the assistants, appreciators and exponents. And though one may be required to pursue an activity outside the home for a very good reason, it can become complementary to the artistic practice of homemaking.

Home can be a haven of peace and harmony if the homemaker finds the middle path of compassion and love for everyone who lives in the house-community, including him or herself. By bringing rhythm into daily life, the balance of sharing will become more equal. By sleeping and waking more wholesomely, a renewed energy for life will arise. By eating together, a new recognition of each other will grow so that mutual support can be maintained. And by celebrating festivals and marking seasons, we will be able to regain a healthy relationship to nature and to the world, living once again in the present and slowing down the illusory speed of time.

3.

Relationships

Warming

A warm and friendly home is founded on love. Yet love is a mystery to most of us because it is something which, when we think about it, becomes rather elusive. When we apply our feelings to it, it becomes more accessible. But if an attempt is made to express it in words or deeds it comes into its own and fills our actions with warmth and purpose. Thus loving and warming are close companions, which can best be grasped by relating them, as with breathing, to the first stages of life.

We have seen how, at the moment of birth, breathing begins and an exchange takes place between the individual and the world. Activity is begun. At this same moment the need arises for contact, which continues until the end of our life on earth. Though the act of breathing is the very first independent action, what follows is a renewed dependency on someone or something other than self. For breathing to continue there must be air, and for contact to be sustained, there must be another person or thing to which to relate.

This need for human warmth is very obvious in a newborn baby. In olden times, babies were swaddled as soon as they were born as though imitating the constrictions of the womb, but also to ensure a sheath of warmth around the vulnerable little child. After all, the womb is a very warm place to be! Nowadays, it is not unusual to refrain from bathing the infant for the first few days so that it can absorb the fats with which it emerged from the womb, and which assist its primary physical need for warmth. We recognize that at birth the baby should remain as close as possible to the mother's or father's body. Modern midwives will see that the baby is placed naked against the bare skin of mother and father so that the first contact can form a natural and close bonding. It is common knowledge that a warm baby sleeps well, that a cold baby may be fractious, and that too much warmth can raise the infant's temperature, causing a fever. It has even been suggested that one of the causes of cot-death is from a rapidly fluctuating environmental temperature. From this we can conclude that holding on to regulated warmth is not something that can function entirely without outside assistance.

In the animal kingdom the young are generally born into nests. The parent creatures spend quite a long time, prior to dropping their young, in search of a suitably safe place. They then rearrange it or reconstruct it to become the best and most protective shelter. The use of this den, nest, or lair, will be for longer or shorter periods, depending on the speed of development of the offspring. The higher the animal, the longer the young spends in the care of its parent, though they may move away from the original shelter of birth.

The human species, however, does not exactly nest-build, but we create homes, places where warmth can be generated, houses which shelter us and can offer protection from undesirable alien elements. Within a warm home, what is known and cherished can flourish. What is cold and frightening can be left outside a sturdy front door. Our use of a home usually continues for the whole of our natural life.

Generally speaking, babies and little children spend a lot of time in the home. They sleep, eat, play and explore their close environment, only gradually extending their interest and curiosity further afield. The small child cannot easily grasp concepts beyond the immediate home environment. Only with time does the sphere of knowledge widen as the young child grows in years, learning and experience.

Throughout this time of learning, the parents are usually closely related and involved in the developments taking place.

During these early years, just as the process of warming needs support in order to be sustained, so does warmth in the immediate vicinity of the child need nurturing and fostering. This can most successfully be carried out by the parents at home because they usually know and love their children, and the environment can be kept familiar and stable. It must, however, be acknowledged that the necessity for a child to attend a crèche, or be cared for by someone else during the day, has become very common practice, but it is generally the happiest and most secure arrangement for the child to remain at home. In point of fact, this desire for warmth, familiarity and security stays with us throughout life. We seek congenial companions, situations of mutual benefit, and work that we can enjoy, and if we can find all these things then we experience an inner blossoming of warmth.

Physically too, the need for warmth continues throughout life. Warmth in the human body works within the circulation of the blood, which is in constant flow and gently heats every part of our organism, but it does not become entirely independent from the temperature outside. Unlike animals, human beings need clothes. From birth it takes a few years for the body temperature to become individualized and to be regulated by our inner personality. The individualized needs of warmth are also reflected in the temperature levels we maintain in our homes, which clearly depend upon personal preference.

Warmth is not only a physical necessity. We also need a warm atmosphere in which to unfold. We are more relaxed and can usually function better if we are with people we love and trust. In an atmosphere of disapproval or suspicion we tend to freeze and become rather stiff and unemotive.

We do not dare to show our feelings and keep to ourselves what moves in our hearts.

Movement invariably generates warmth, and human interaction depends upon something moving from one person to another, or between a person and the world, or between a person and an object. Such movements also generate a quality of soul warmth. This warmth-bringing activity is created in the life body and can be called the *process of warming* because it regulates our physical temperature, as well as the warmth of our moods of soul. Another way of describing this process is to see it as something that allows us to share the more intimate aspects of our personality. Needless to say, this sharing has to include cooling down, as well as warming up. For example, when chatting agreeably with friends, the movement of warmth that flows from one to the other can become almost tangible. But if a disagreement arises, the movement could be described as being withdrawn and a chill may descend upon the group. The close relationship of loving warmth around one and warmth in the individual human being starts to become apparent when we discover the connection of personality and warmth. It can be seen in the way we maintain our contacts. Some people are reserved, holding back from creating relationships too rapidly, preferring to keep things cool. Others enthusiastically enter into friendships and can sometimes just as quickly discard them. However, in every instance, a relationship asks of one to connect with someone else, with something other than self, and in so doing, the warmth of involvement comes into being.

From infancy human beings are dependent not only on their parents but also on the universe. It is because of this fact of dependency that we are able to learn about the world. We learn that we are part of our environment because we are subjectively inserted into the world. We need its air, light, warmth and food in order to survive. But we can also form objective concepts about it because, though we are in *intimate relationship* with it, we can *stand outside* it by virtue of our power of thought. And because we can think about things, we can understand them, and this forms the basis for our love of life. Whatever love we have for the world and what is in it, is founded on our ability to understand what we meet. In the home, that place where we can safely experiment with our first relationships and where trust is the ground under our feet, is where it all begins.

From this warm security, we begin, right in infancy, to understand the world by imitating not only what is present as outer activity, but also what moves within the souls and thoughts of the people around us. We are, of course, most deeply and lastingly touched by our parents' attitudes, thoughts and feelings and later by siblings and other close relatives, but as we widen our relationships these influences also expand.

Little children usually meet the world with an enthusiasm that is heart-warming. They eagerly expect everyone and everything to be wise and also good. A small child who is suspicious and frightened may have suffered some form of hurt or betrayal. It could even stem from such an apparently small thing as disinterest or boredom that may have been the general tone of the toddler's environment at home. It is a well-known fact that the cause of deprivation and the root of delinquency, as well as other moral difficulties, can often be traced to an early childhood home environment of rejection, abuse, intolerance or disinterest. These are extreme examples of an atmosphere devoid of warmth. It should also be noted that an environment filled with too much heat of passion can be equally unhealthy. It leads to heavily weighted and painful human relationships.

To sustain good human contact in order to create a warm and loving home, means to pay attention to our relationships, and this requires a certain self-knowledge and self-

control. Our feeling life can be strong and compelling as
well as being so very varied. Moreover, we can at times feel
that being at home, which is a relatively small environment,
can hamper us from expressing our inner desires and aims
sufficiently. Sometimes we may even find ourselves taking
this out on our dependants or partners. It is not uncommon
to feel a certain frustration with oneself and the home,
finding life stifling and almost too confining in its intimacy.
This may be because the relationship of home and self are
not in harmony. The swing from sympathy towards
wanting the best for everyone, and unhappiness in the way
we think we ought to achieve this, is perhaps too marked.
Perhaps we expect ourselves to be magically good at sustaining relationships, or conversely feel that they really
ought to look after themselves. This may be because our
sympathy towards self and the other person fluctuates rather
too rapidly, creating disharmony and quarrels. Yet sympathy, if properly directed, can give access to another
person's inner qualities. By entering that precious place a
true understanding of another's point of view and character
can arise.

The physical and social warmth that we encounter
throughout life is so effective that its lack can lie at the root
of illnesses relating to the blood and circulation. A physically warm home will not only help to prevent illnesses
such as fever or inflammations, but if this warmth is lifted
into the social sphere it will create an atmosphere that will
teach us how to sustain good relationships. The path of our
destiny will naturally bring its ups and downs and the more
warmth we can call up from a happy and secure childhood,
the better able will we be to cope with the mood-swings
that will occur as part of our adult daily life.

Most of our ordinary relationships are based on subjective or objective feelings towards other people or things.
We swing between the two all the time but usually rather
unconsciously. Subjectivity means to involve our feelings in

our thoughts and actions, whereas objectivity means to disengage our feelings and relate to things by thinking about them. We identify these complementary faculties of soul as sympathy and antipathy. To the homemaker, using these qualities wisely is helpful in avoiding favouritism or indifference, both of which have the potential to damage a warm home.

Sympathy and Antipathy

Sympathy and antipathy can be described as our social and anti-social forces. Some things attract us, some things make us retreat from them. The same holds good in our relationships. We are drawn to some people, repelled by others and often cannot find a really good explanation for this. We just feel sympathetic to some things and instinctively reject others, and this activity of sympathy and antipathy lies at the root of our social dispositions. To control or develop these faculties the individual must take charge. Our true inner nature, our ego, has the power to direct our capacity to love in a way that rises above our instincts or our moods.

Sympathy, which is instinctive attraction, can create a deeper and more intimate understanding of a person's feelings, but it can also draw one towards too close a contact that can make one want to take sides. Then objectivity is lost and feelings can run very high, making solutions become more evasive. Sometimes, when a person is ill, too much sympathy can make them feel even worse and delay the healing process. Sympathy, though very necessary in its rightful place, can create a hothouse atmosphere and cause complications where a touch of cooling antipathy, or objectivity could put everything right again. Antipathy, however, can lead to rejection. It can be the cause of criticism and cold comfort. In an attempt to be clear and objective, one can lean too much towards an intellectual and theoretical method when dealing with people and situations. In its rightful place, antipathy keeps one cool in emotional moments, but it can make one cold-blooded in situations that would perhaps need warmth and involvement in order to understand them fully.

Sympathy and antipathy are neither love nor hate. They are simply faculties of soul. They influence our relationships and work as balancing factors that lie within the control of human consciousness. A gentle and conscious movement between these two soul qualities is a step towards learning about what love really is, though to talk of love means to enter into very deep waters. We generally use the word rather lightly, giving it connotations belonging to sympathy. We use the word hate intending it to mean the opposite of love, when in point of fact what we actually mean is rather more a mood of antipathy or rejection.

Our moods of soul work actively in all relationships. It would be true to say that most people long for friendships so that they can share their joys and woes. We need each other to carry life's burdens, to laugh together and also to learn from each other. It is usually far easier to bear a rebuke from a friend than from a mere acquaintance, however tactfully it may have been delivered. It is on the warmth of relationships that self-knowledge can grow.

A sound relationship may begin from a natural sympathy, but it can just as easily grow out of antipathy, which has been consciously overcome. It is possible that sympathy can dry up. It is also possible that conquering antipathy by decisively working at recognizing and cherishing another person can make a true and lasting friendship. Homemakers are frequently faced with precisely this challenge. We do not always see eye to eye with everyone else. And yet an atmosphere of antipathy at home is too cold, and one of too much sympathy is too cloying. If it were left to nature we would swing between these two states of soul, and maybe create rather too variable a mood within the home. But generally an effort is made to keep on an even keel, and from this attempt a new quality of soul can arise—that of *empathy*.

Empathy

In homemaking this quality has been working for a long time but it has been given its rightful place only recently. It is the ability that makes some people good listeners. They become able to pay attention in a very particular way when listening. It is as though a part of their soul opens up and then reflects the words they are hearing, as well as the meaning. Taking part in such a conversation, where listener and speaker are equally engaged, allows problems to be shared, and so they become less burdensome to carry. Something wordless is conveyed that opens the way for a solution to arise and yet no advice has actually been given.

Empathy is more than fellow feeling. It is an intensely active quality that can only work when one practises self-lessness. It disappears the moment one's own agenda enters the picture. It is the gift of being able to identify with another person's circumstances. To be able to do this and to experience someone else's point of view without judgement or criticism—this is empathy. Using sympathy and antipathy alone as the measure for what someone else suffers creates the potential for illusion because it works only out of a subjective or objective standpoint. This cannot answer every difficulty in life. Homemakers faced with the question of suffering, the problems of relationships and other situations of destiny, will gradually discover that mediating wisely is very much easier if listening with empathy is the starting point. When relationships need repairing, to begin from one's own point of view tends to lead to misjudgement and mistaken conclusions. To patch up a quarrel or to mend friendships requires a focus, which is neither cold, nor clinical in its objectivity. Warm approval of the persons involved, coupled with clear observation of their situation, can only be achieved if one sets one's own agenda aside and enters into their state of mind. Though this may sound very hard and even an imposition on one's freedom of self-expression, the feeling of inner peace that arises is quite tangible when one makes the attempt at empathizing.

Another aspect that homemakers may find to be part of their task is to act as arbitrator between members of the house-community. This is a delicate matter, needing warmth, but also clear perceptions as to what is actually causing the dissent. To discover the causes calls up the power of empathy so that one can attempt to interiorize the obvious distress, observe its effect upon oneself and so move towards a satisfactory solution for all. This can best come about if a warm interest towards everyone in the home is cultivated. Homeliness and cosiness depend upon this kind of enthusiasm for one's fellow human beings because people find themselves relaxing in an atmosphere generated by real interest.

Interest

Interest awakens empathy. It is the prime motivator for learning about life and the world and our fellow human beings. It paves the way to self-knowledge, an attribute without which working in the home could become a rather difficult and emotional career. Without interest, relation-ships would die. It causes us to hold back sympathy and antipathy in order to be able to enter into another person's being. It makes us relate selflessly and from this small sacrifice we can learn something new about other people and ourselves. It frees us to become aware of the other person who hides behind the mask of a persona, which is how most of us choose to present ourselves to the world. This psychological phenomenon relates to our position in life, our status, our sex, and our self-esteem. We create many different masks, (or personas), each according to the relevant situation in which we find ourselves. And we usually know which mask to put on depending on the people and events we encounter throughout our daily experience. Using inappropriate masks, or finding ourselves with too few to suit every occasion, is the lot of those human beings who suffer disabilities. Mental illness may mean that inappropriate masks are chosen or forced upon us through an inability to select. We can also find ourselves stuck behind a particular mask, unable to express our true individuality.

Because working at home requires so many masks that appear to be very similar, the homemaker will discover that they can be used with subtlety. One may be a mother, a father, a teacher, or mentor. One may be cook, cleaner, administrator, consultant, gardener, and much more. Each area has its appropriate mask, which one can don as required. The more there are, the more flexible and interesting the role as homemaker becomes. The more there are, the more objectively and clearly can the home-maker work within the given tasks.

There are three principle masks from which we can choose that provide a background for coping creatively with the role that life offers us. On these we can place all the other diverse aspects that we want to use. The first is to portray: *I am what I am*; the second portrays: *I am what I have;* and the third: *I am what I do.*

The first mask is by far the most broad in its spectrum. On the basic premise that one is confidently oneself, one can fit all the lesser masks of life experience, careers, or tasks one may take up as the years pass by. To be only an expression of one's position or possessions, or merely an image of one's chosen profession could be very confining, and inhibit freedom of choice where masks are concerned. Being limited by the name of a role, or having to keep up appearances, are two of the prime reasons that Ahriman and

Lucifer offer as excuses for avoiding the demanding yet fulfilling task of homemaking.

When one observes toddlers and their very straightforward approach to life, one can experience a lack of inhibition, but also a certain refreshing freedom in their uncomplicated honest approach. They simply *are*. This is a lesson that teaches us that *before* we had or did, we were an expression of self. Later, as children grow into adulthood, they learn and so acquire many and varied masks. But these are all worn on the backdrop of the self. The self can always shine through, and it is this identity that calls up interest from others with whom one comes into contact. Then, no matter what the age or status, one has found freedom of expression.

Because homemakers are not only concerned with children but also with other age groups, making a home that has warmth means to show an interest in the masks that others wear but also to allow them to be taken off in an atmosphere free of judgement. Interest can be the way to form a space for this revelation of self. When such trust is achieved, the possibility to meet the rest of one's life with empathy may gradually also be attained. Confidence and trust in one another are the flowers that grow on interest, creating the atmosphere we long to have at home.

Atmosphere

Just as breathing depends upon air, the warmth in the atmosphere at home depends upon how relationships are conducted and expressed. A quarrelsome situation is not very inviting. Usually it causes all but the protagonists to leave the room! Sometimes it goes underground and festers. Things that should really be no problem can become issues, and jobs that are actually quite pleasant can suddenly become onerous. Then apathy follows and smothers all spontaneity and fun in life. In places of employment, the situation just described would be dealt with by the management, since discord creates a poor work ethic. In the home, someone must step in to resolve the knots we create for each other in life, and this task is certainly part of homemaking, though others in the home may also help to bring harmony again. A home can no more flourish under strife than can an office or a building site.

Children will usually be an excellent barometer of the atmosphere. In a quarrelsome environment they eat less, sleep poorly, (often with nightmares), and cannot settle down to real play. Sometimes this expresses itself by professing boredom or whining, as well as attention-seeking. They seem to feel chilled and rejected by the atmosphere around them. Old people too, can become insecure and anxious if people around them are at odds with each other. An attitude of encouragement, interest and enthusiasm can overcome many obstacles. Even illness and depression can be borne more cheerfully in a loving and caring atmosphere.

We recognize the home as a living organism, and we see that the body as a whole must be in harmony with its parts. Just as a diseased organ, or any illness at all, makes one feel very uncomfortable, so does the home suffer an equal discomfort if its members cannot get along with each other. The way forward is the practice of empathy. This is not so easy if one is too closely linked with a particular disagreement, but the effort alone will bring some ease and will pay off in the end. Almost everything we wish to master requires practice, and homemaking is not exempt from this law! Just as learning the violin usually starts off rather painfully with squeaks of the bow and aches in the arms and fingers, so too does homemaking often begin in a similar clumsy fashion. But with practice, beautiful music is so often the result, as homemaking becomes a true expression of the social art.

The atmosphere at home can be very like the weather:

we can make it sunny, warm and pleasant, or fill it with the breeze of enthusiasm. It can be clouded and chilly, darkened by ill-will, or it can be invigorated by a thunderstorm. A thunderstorm is not always a bad thing because it can clear the way and make space for a fresh start. But anger should be used sparingly, and only when one is as sure as is humanly possible that one has understood the situation correctly. If control is lost, which is a very human failing, then an apology and the hope of forgiveness can open a channel for warmth to flow in a more even way once more.

Just as the weather can be so hot that it becomes oppressive, so too can passion and too much personal involvement between members of the house-community dominate the home. Emotions that are too strongly felt, opinions that are too passionately adhered to, can make others feel that they are outside the magic circle. It tends to stifle initiative and create a heavy, burdensome atmosphere. Very small children and fragile older people can experience this as a kind of violence towards their tender inner selves. It makes them insecure in their relationship towards people and things. Enthusiasm, on the other hand, includes everyone. It draws people together, carrying them along until their own inner fire can be kindled. It is like the warmth of the spring sun. In contrast, a cool, analytical approach to life can be as refreshing as iced water on a hot day, or it can chill the soul, damping down the fires of enthusiasm. Too much caution can be like winter all the year round.

The human centre for warmth, interest and enthusiasm is in the heart, that very faithful organ that beats on steadily for the whole of one's life on earth. The homemaker can be that heartbeat of warmth and enthusiasm if interest and encouragement work together in harmony. Then sympathy and antipathy become creative acts and people will enjoy living together, rather than side by side under one roof. An atmosphere of interest and enthusiasm makes it possible to talk freely to one another, to enjoy discussion and to share the humour and drama of life. Conversations build sound relationships. Unless we talk to each other openly and without fear of negative criticism we will find it hard to get to know each other. An atmosphere that engenders warmth towards anyone who enters, be they strangers, guests or friends, is truly a home.

Making a Home

Making a home requires first and foremost the interest to do so, and then a house in which to create it. Whatever the type, size or shape of house, the first thing we meet is the entrance, the doorway, hall, passage or kitchen. This first encounter tells us so much about those who inhabit the home. It is, one might say, the first greeting that we hope will be warm and inviting. There are many ingredients that help to create this first impression, such as colour, light and temperature. The décor that pleases the eye, however, is only part of this special experience of feeling instantly at home. What really lies behind it is the love that is given to the functional aspects of the home. We show this in the fact that care is taken to hang the coats on a stand or hooks, and to have a practical place on which to leave one's outdoor shoes. Behind this attention to practical detail lies love for all that is friendly and beautiful about our earth. This conveys itself wordlessly not only to the visitor but also to the tired or happy, sad or noisy home-comer. Moving on from the entrance into particular rooms offers changes in atmosphere because each room has its own special part to play within the ambience of the home.

If one chooses to work with the social art then to cultivate particular qualities relevant to particular rooms can be an exciting challenge. And if this variety is consciously cherished it will be noticeable how people will feel and talk to each other differently in the various rooms. One can make use of this quite deliberately in tense or tender moments. Bedroom, bathroom or sitting-room each have their functions, but also their ambience and social possibilities. If conversation is the foundation of developing and sustaining relationships, then cultivating places where we can talk freely is very important. *How* we speak to one another matters very much. Most things, both palatable and unpalatable, can be said if the right moment, place and note is found. Within a conducive atmosphere, questions can be asked, observations made and confidences shared in the certainty that they will be met with understanding.

Making a home includes the recognition and acknowledgement of everyone's needs. It is fairly well known that children flourish best in surroundings that suit their particular phase of development. It is equally important for people of all ages to be in a comfortable and appropriate environment. Home should meet the individual inner and outer needs. Because we want to share in creating the atmosphere, this does not mean we have to leave ourselves out of it! Everyone has their own idea of what makes a warm and friendly home and this includes the homemaker who is responsible for making the home that suits all who live in it.

Part of homemaking is to pay attention to the purely practical aspects of keeping warm. In many climates some form of heating is necessary, in others air-conditioning can be very useful. To adjust to one's environment is, however, the most energy-efficient and also usually the healthiest way of staying comfortable. Temperature levels are, of course, very individual. Moreover, they affect our concentration span, so that different temperatures will encourage different activities, and it is therefore important to become sensitive to the levels of warmth required. We tend to want to go to sleep when it is too warm. The same thing happens when it is excessively cold. A middle range of warmth allows the maximum relaxation coupled with the greatest alertness of mind. This means dressing appropriately to the outer temperature rather than over heating or cooling down the house itself.

Clothing

Added to the physical temperature within the home is the quality of warmth generated by the clothes that we wear. The subject of clothing is an aspect of homemaking that we sometimes neglect because we place it in the area of individual taste, rather than seeing that our body heat can influence our ability to think and concentrate, as well as our ability to act appropriately. Then what we wear to keep warm or cool becomes something of importance.

We wear clothes not only to maintain an even body temperature but also to give expression to our personality. Generally, people wear what they feel good in and have a very individual taste in style, and colour, and so on. But we could pay just as much attention to the fabrics as to the design since they provide us with the comfort to conduct our lives in the way we wish, or hinder us by making us irritable and affecting our objectivity.

The process of warming needs to be constant in order to maintain a sense of well-being. The fabrics worn affect this constancy. Natural fibres such as wool, linen and cotton allow the skin to breathe in a wholesome way. Perspiration cools the body temperature and acts as a regulator. Artificial fibres can prevent this cooling process by blocking the flow of air to the skin so that perspiration cannot dry, or cannot be secreted. Then one feels too hot, or too cold, one shivers, or gets irritable. This is how our consciousness is distracted by something as apparently insignificant as the fabric of our clothing.

Parents rearing small children will generally find that clothing of natural fibres gives their children greater physical comfort. It is in the home that most clothes are washed, dried and generally cared for. Therefore it is reasonable to assume that the homemaker has some say in what is acquired. To decide on appropriate clothing may be relatively simple where small children are concerned, but adolescents usually enjoy being in the height of fashion and like to choose their own clothes. Unfortunately, fashion clothing is more often made from artificial fibres than not, and the friction caused by the fibres against the skin sets up static electricity, which can cause a subliminal irritability. This affects daily life, and it will happen to everyone who wears artificial fabrics. Different people can cope with varying levels of static so there can be no recipe, only sound common sense and a practical experience of the levels of tolerance. However, wearing artificial fabrics whilst doing the household chores may be one of the reasons for a high level of irritability. One needs to be comfortable to work hard, not distracted by minutely shivering skin surfaces.

It is at home that one can relax and be oneself, so clothing that expresses a particular mask or persona of the day need not be worn. One can just unwind and put on whatever is most comfortable, no longer needing to make a statement of intent. Much can be learned about our state of mind, mood or desires by the clothes we wear. Our taste expresses an aspect of the masks we choose to don. If one becomes sensitive to this then one can offer the appropriate support or help, whichever is the most needed at the time. It may be that a person can be helped by a particular kind of dress as a protection for a tender state of mind. Often old people need warm soft clothing that is loose in style, as do babies, who also need soft warm fabrics. Adolescents need clothes behind which to hide until they have found their own beautiful selves. Adults in general wear clothes to suit mood or job or body temperature. Jewels, bright colours, sombre browns and blacks, all tell something about the wearer. Changing clothes can be an expression of altered intentions, or an expression of bodily need, for example, when one is working up a fever caused by incipient illness.

Illness

Disease upsets the process of warming by attacking the life body, and this usually shows in a change of our body temperature. We develop a fever, or get the shivers, perspire heavily or develop a dry, hot skin, become flushed or very pale. We feel decidedly out of sorts with ourselves and the world in general and just want to go home to be spoiled and cared for.

Homemaking once included knowledge of children's diseases, first aid, and treatment of common ailments. This was usually passed on from grandmother, to mother, to daughter. In general, illness was recognized as a state of vulnerability, and in homes where poverty was not the overriding factor, illness was treated with great respect. Even in the poorer homes, special attention was afforded the sufferers wherever possible. Apart from medical treatment, patients were given special food and quiet companionship; they were kept in clean, aired rooms, provided with extra bedclothes where necessary and were generally cosseted. Once on the mend, a time was set aside for recuperation, the sufferer only gradually returning to full working capacity.

In comparison, illness today receives remarkably little attention. Usually one visits the doctor to request a fast cure, maybe goes to bed, and as soon as the fever has abated, one is up and back to work. It is as though we want to ignore any sign of weakness. We seem to feel the need to be in full control of our destiny and our life style at all times. In general, we tend to dislike, and even fear illness.

It is interesting to become aware of the reasons behind the fact that one gets ill. It is often when life becomes burdensome in some way that the body reacts by making us feel the need to shut down and go to bed. We withdraw into ourselves, sleep a great deal, and so at last find the time to do a bit of stock-taking as to the state our life is in at present. Often, on recovery, if time has been allowed for the illness to run its course, we feel better than we did before the illness struck! Sometimes we even feel up to taking decisions which prior to the sickness we had neither the energy nor the insight to make. Illness often strikes us down when we need to make new relationships, either to life, to other people or towards our own inner self. Our wise psyche places us into an anti-social situation that others are called upon to meet with their social forces of sympathy. In this reciprocal moment a new balance can be created and old concepts can be reformed. For this development to happen, however, someone else needs to be present other than oneself. Someone needs to *be there*.

Just as human beings cannot live without a heart, so too is the home impeded in its main function from becoming a living, warm organism if it lacks a homemaker. *Being there* is essential. It is really rather difficult to achieve this effect from a distance. But it can be the cause of a great deal of stress and pressure of conscience to feel in the position of being in two places at once. Many homemakers have to suffer this because they are at the same time the bread-winners of the home. There are no easy answers to this problem. How to care for the sick at home when one cannot be there all the time highlights this dilemma. But perhaps it depends on one's being really *there* when one does manage to be at home. It is heart-warming to see health and vitality returning to the patient if one is able and willing to be available with one's full attention. To those who suffer long-term illnesses, the presence of the home-maker can make all the difference to their sense of well-being whilst coping with the vulnerability that usually accompanies poor health. Once again, empathy helps to make the nursing easier because we can perceive what the patient and the illness require in order to restore good health. For instance, some people need physical warmth, yet a quiet, cool approach, whilst others will want fresh air and lots of cheerful company in order to recover quickly. What most of us have in common, however, is a longing for the gentle, warm and loving support of another human being, which is, in the end, the main source of healing.

If illness can gain some personal space in a very busy life for the purposes already expressed, then it comes to us for a good reason and its source may well be something other than merely a bacterial or viral infection. There are expressions in our language that hint at common ailments, yet are used to express certain states of mind or emotions. When something is too much to deal with we say: 'I can't digest all that', 'That's too much to swallow', 'It's more than I can carry', 'It's a pain in the neck'. When our life style is not as it really should be, a stomach-ache, sore throat, backache or migraine can show us that we are not dealing with our problems effectively. We are, in fact, struggling inwardly with our own self-development.

Something comes about through illness that affects the whole of one's life. If we observe objectively and without fear, we can see that common diseases such as mumps, measles or whooping-cough bring something new into the development of children. Perhaps they start to grow physically, or a new quality of thinking can be observed, once they have recovered. More intelligible speech can also be the result of these ailments. They seem to bring something new into the pattern of development. And yet, we can ask: where and why does illness arise? We can also ask: why do we need to suffer in order to change?

Through illness we are given the opportunity to learn that this life we are living is not the only one. Somewhere, deep in our subconscious, we suspect that this may be true. There are people today who have been through illnesses that have called up memories from past lives. They gleaned from what is known as near-death experiences that living has a purpose. It is the sum of our experiences, deeds and thoughts: it is our *karma*—carried from one life into the next incarnation, and on into the next, in accordance with human evolutionary development. Illnesses in particular can be seen in this developmental light, but so too is all life experience essential as we weave the karmic threads that we bring with us into what we call our life on earth.

Karma

All human beings bring with them at birth an innate knowledge of what they want to learn in this lifetime. This desire is based on what has gone before in a previous life. What will happen in our future life depends on how we meet and tackle our present earth life. What is past cannot be altered; this is something we know and experience daily. Once a deed is done it can be changed, developed or denied but it can never be undone. However, what we do with what we have learned from the past is our free choice. Freedom lies in taking up our karma, the path of life that we have chosen. If we have accepted our destiny with courage, then what follows is a tendency to find life moving along a little more smoothly. There may even be less illness along the way if we can meet our destiny positively!

In the normal course of life we do not often think about the fact that illness may strike in order to teach a lesson. Nor do we necessarily think that the person we meet and with whom perhaps we choose to share our lives, and have children, may not have been encountered by mere chance. Even real destiny we can fail to recognize with full conscious knowledge. Yet children often express an experience of reincarnation quite naturally and easily, such as dreaming of when they were big, just as old people remember the past. It is becoming more and more common to feel that we know someone at the first meeting. And yet, it would appear that at present we are quite undecided about what to think regarding reincarnation and the forming of destiny.

Security and confidence in life exist because we can experience continuity. A loss of memory creates deep uncertainty. If we convince ourselves that we live only this one life, then we are in danger of losing our reason for self-development. We have now reached a stage in the development of humanity where we are open to regain knowledge of the fact of reincarnation. We can continue our progress with greater conscious knowledge if we recognize this to be the reason for so many experiences that shape and structure our developing individuality.

Just as we sleep and wake and sleep again, so too have we lived successive lives and are on the way to further lives for the sake of our development. The purpose is for human beings to learn to love in all its fullness. Just as the sculptor smoothes the rough stone until it has the beautiful likeness of a god, so does the individual spirit, or ego, hone and shape the soul and body. And so, within these manifold lives on earth appear the necessities that we meet in order to learn to love completely. This does not happen without some suffering and pain, hence the illnesses and obstacles that we meet in our lives.

This challenge lays a foundation for the task of home-making and offers an aim, which makes the work both creative and rewarding. The more love and acceptance that we offer to the task, the more will we deepen our experience of its central place in human life on earth. To know that the love and concern that we can extend within the home comes out of a past endeavour begun in a previous life, is good grounds for generating positivity! Providing continuity, enjoying the daily activities, and meeting the challenges because they are what we have chosen to meet, makes homemaking a reality in relation to the forming of a renewed social life.

People who have become aware of reincarnation are sometimes prone to being rather drawn towards the future, tending to worry about what might be coming to them the next time around. But it is equally important to become aware of influences from the life before our birth. During this time we are already sorting out what we need to experience in order to learn that which we know we must master. We work all this out together with our angel and other angelic beings, who accompany us on our way to reach the true goal of humanity. Once we have understood the reality of the influences of the spiritual world as well as our own input into this mighty task of learning to love, then our attitude to our relationships will alter. We will be more conscious of the control we have, not over *what* we meet, but *how* we meet it.

What we *think* has very much more effect on the people around us than we usually notice. Equally, how we relate to others touches everyone. The thoughts, actions and intentions, as well as the atmosphere created by our parents, form the physical basis of our lives. These lay down the inclinations towards illnesses, especially of a psychological nature, but also physical ailments, which we develop later on in life. This is why we often blame our weaknesses on our unfortunate parents, even though they are not responsible for all of them! If we can so affect each other's early development, then the consequences will live in us throughout our life on earth. To carry such responsibility needs knowledge and skills. It is therefore necessary to learn to see where Lucifer and Ahriman interfere. They work in our inclination either to ignore the past and focus on the future only, or in our hankering after what used to be so nice in the past. Lucifer persuades us to be forever seeking what is new, never really being satisfied with what we have, and Ahriman wants us to resent any changes. He would have us try to keep everything the same.

This makes it very clear that creating a warm and vibrant

home that embraces past, present and future is basic to a healthy life. It is at its best when it can include old traditions as well as new developments, maintain steady and tried relationships, as well as new and inspiring encounters. Children can flourish in homes that encompass such attitudes and aspirations, and the elderly and frail can find security, comfort and perhaps even new thoughts and feelings to add to their precious memories.

Creating a home means to be at the cutting edge of karmic events. Nothing is too small or too big that it cannot happen at home. This means that one can learn to nurture the destiny of each individual in such a way that everyone can accept what comes towards him or her in life with positivity, and that each will know how best to create new and helpful karma for a future life. What homemakers can accomplish by means of a positive approach will be of benefit to everyone in the home. When we begin the difficult task of practising devotion, positivity and compassion we will be starting on the road towards practising real and universal love.

Love

In everything that lives, love finds a means of expression. The world was created from heavenly love and so will find its spiritual home in the love that humanity extends towards creation. As yet we are still struggling to find the real meaning of this mighty revelation of soul and spirit, which is only given to human beings to express. That sentiment which we call love today, is really only a very small part of its vast and creative activity. Generally speaking, we would love to love our life and work, and so in every walk of life and in every work situation we search for meaning. Human beings generally want to know that what they do is necessary and also creative within society as a whole.

Sometimes homemakers find themselves asking: Do I

love my life? Am I doing what I love? And the answers will vary because each person is different. What can result from an honest searching of the soul is the discovery that we make a home in order to create security, to nurture self-confidence and to find self-esteem. With regard to the question of love, we cannot always give a straight answer. We may discover that we have probably learned about love from the way in which we were reared and from what we met as expressions of love within our early childhood environment. If this is true, then homemaking becomes a very serious and worthwhile effort. It is a task vital for the world today, because it can set into motion a renewed attempt at finding the meaning and expression of love, based on an understanding of karma and reincarnation. Home is the place where one can learn to accept one's destiny and gain the tools to work out of free choice.

We would love to love what we do but sometimes find it hard because the apparent freedom of choice seems so limited within the structure of the home. But in those moments where acceptance relaxes the tensions, and resentment is stilled, then a warmth flows between members of the house-community and for that precious time each person can be experienced as a striving and creative human being. The consequent flow of warmth that streams towards the homemaker is the outcome of such special moments.

It is by working towards a conscious control of sympathy and antipathy that such experiences can become more frequent. Warm affection is a great deal more trustworthy than fluctuating emotions. We are well on the road to mastering Lucifer's drive towards strong opinions and Ahriman's attempts to narrow us down into efficient, manipulative housekeepers, if we enjoy meeting the challenges that a serious search for equanimity presents.

Love fills the home when interest in each other's destiny is cultivated. Relationships can flourish, grow and change, disasters can be weathered, and pain can be patiently borne and overcome in the warmth of understanding. Reflecting without judgement, listening with empathy and acting with enthusiasm will bring love nearer to us as an achievable spiritual activity.

4.

The Artistic Environment

Nourishing

The process of nourishing is part of the law of life. From the first breath, followed by protective warmth from the parent, the baby finds the sustaining breast and a sense of total comfort and security eases the infant's arrival in the world. A well fed baby is a delightfully milky bundle of warmth.

Human beings fill a large part of their daily life with the question of nourishment. When we take a closer look at the process itself, we find that it is not only food that nourishes us but that there is something more to nutrition than mere physical substance. The plants get their main nourishment from light, air and water. Animals feed off plants, as well as other animals. They too need light and air and water. Nothing feeds off the physical alone. Human beings are unique in that, though fed by plants and animals, by light, air and water, we seek for other sources of nourishment. We require nourishing of the soul and spirit in order to develop our full potential.

Just as understanding the fourfold nature of the human being helps to establish rhythm in daily life, seeing our threefold nature, which is another way of comprehending the human constitution, can help in finding appropriate forms of nourishment. The body, as we know, is physical and dense, and we need it in order to live on the earth and to comprehend how the material world works. Because of its material nature it is the most vulnerable part of us with the least resistance to outer influences. It can become ill, and it needs a great deal of attention and care, which includes healthy food. And yet, this clumsy physical body houses the human spirit and is the visible servant of the soul. The soul is the bearer of our thoughts and feelings, our moods, and artistic inclinations and with its mobility and flexibility we make friends, learn, and express ourselves. What feeds the soul is art and beauty, and imagination.

The human spirit is indestructible. Whereas the physical body dies and returns to the material world, allowing the human soul to expand after death, the human spirit endures. The spirit irrefutably *is*, filling the soul with purpose, knowledge and love, but because of the vulnerability of the body and the sensitivity of the soul, the spirit can be separated from its companions. What the spirit seeks as food is the expression of truth, goodness and love in human deeds and thoughts.

By understanding the threefold human being as *body, soul and spirit*, one can see that each aspect requires a very different kind of nourishment and that a single one of the three can suffer deprivation or malnutrition, whilst the others may be well fed. Where proper attention is given to all three, especially throughout childhood, they can work together to provide good health, a rich soul life and a potential for spiritual striving.

However, in general, we muddle along in life, paying little or no attention to the startling fact that we are made up of three distinctly different aspects, all working together. We live as we please. We eat, read, watch films, play video games or whatever takes our fancy, and we work at our jobs. We also sleep and spend time socializing. Perhaps on occasion we go to church, or find a religious direction that gives us a certain feeling of satisfaction. But sometimes we experience a kind of hunger, a feeling of needing some food, which we cannot really identify. It can be as though there is an empty hole in the core of our being. This will not be unfamiliar to the homemaker, who may at times feel a form of frustration and dissatisfaction, which seems to be vague and generalized. Then homemaking can appear as the least fulfilling of vocations.

It is well known that malnutrition in infancy causes sensory disorders, thus inhibiting development. What is less commonly recognized is that if the soul is not properly fed, maladjustment, vandalism, and obsessive behaviour, as well as some emotional disorders, may be the result.

As to nourishing of the spirit, the third and most directive part of the human being, this is sometimes the most subtle and complicated to achieve. In our sincere search for freedom of thought, of speech and of religion, we can find ourselves not knowing how to choose, or what to think. One of the unfortunate results is that children can grow up with a careless and blasé attitude to life. Another problem can be a too rigid adherence to proven dogma, opening up the potential for fear in childhood that may lead to eating disorders. Anorexia and bulimia are becoming an increasing problem. If all three aspects of the human being are to be nourished appropriately, the homemaker needs to learn that nourishment for the soul and spirit is as essential as is a study of nutrition for the body. There are, however, some aspects about nourishing the physical body which are very important to address.

Feeding the Body

Good food is always enjoyable. To sit down to a meal that is made up of one's favourite dishes and sauces has been the basis of social occasions since time immemorial. Feasts were prepared whenever something important occurred. Weddings, baptisms, funerals, state occasions, birthdays, in fact, any happening that people wanted to remember could call for a banquet. Nowadays, within the home, parties take up this important place in life, where the food is always special and great attention is given to its preparation and presentation. Everyone's favourite recipe can be arranged for such events.

However, usually we do not celebrate something every day and so we eat fairly ordinary food, selecting things to which we are accustomed. Moreover, most people are conscious of their health as well as their physical strength and abilities, so much so, that we may have an inclination to devote too much attention to nutrition, therefore believing a variety of theories on the subject of what is healthy. Could this be the voice of Lucifer, enticing us into food fads and persuading us that we should eat only what is pure? Ahriman too, enters the fray, whispering that as long as it has its additional vitamins and minerals, then it must be healthy! With these two voices in our ears, how can we avoid taking our daily food as a commodity that is owed to us, rather than in gratitude for the abundance of the earth, tilled by human hands?

Generally, it would be true to say that people have a varied approach to food, which is usually related to their cultural heritage. The homemaker, who is also often the cook, will be quite familiar with this question of taste! And though one cannot please everyone all the time, one can try to follow the general rule that a balanced diet is the most healthy. Vegetables, proteins and carbohydrates spread evenly throughout the day is the best way of achieving this end. Many excellent books on nutrition and the different values in the various foods can be obtained.

However, in order to manage effective eating habits, it is helpful to understand a few things about the digestive system. The stomach itself is a creature of habit. It likes the food to be familiar and it likes to receive it in a calm and conversational atmosphere. It is very easy to get indigestion whilst eating in a loud, restless or argumentative environment. The palate, on the other hand, enjoys a variety of tastes and smells and is highly stimulated by what the eye beholds. Good cooks address their art to satisfying all these desires.

In child development, attention to the stomach is important. We know that we should introduce solid foods rather carefully. This enhances natural health and strengthens the immune system. Babies are satisfied with very little or no variety in their food and are quite happy to eat the same sort of thing every day. Their very toes literally curl with pleasure. Gradually, as the heavier foods are introduced, a greater variety can also be offered. As children grow older, their tastes change. The young child's eyes light up at foods that the adolescent might consider plain and boring because they prefer spices and colour on their plates. By the time adulthood is reached, all sorts of dishes have become enjoyable and we will be less particular in what we eat. We will probably be more interested in its nutritional value! Elderly people like the foods of by-gone years because they bring back memories.

The relationship between food, taste and memory is not merely nostalgia. Taste stimulates imagination, and healthy, natural and organic foods stimulate life. A lively approach to things can encourage our power of memory. Malnutrition does not help physical development and this in turn affects the activity of the senses so that the impressions that we register in our memory consequently become paler and weaker. Good food in childhood will go a long way to a good memory in adulthood.

In former times we ate food grown locally and organically. Now we eat foods grown all over the world, but we still tend to enjoy fresh produce from our own country. This is because its quality is the most suited to our digestive system, which we discover when abroad and suffering from tourist tummy! The digestive system, as we know, likes familiarity, but it also likes regularity and it works best when fed at the same times every day. This is an important thing to note because we tend towards filling our stomach not only irregularly but also with substances that it may not find digestible. Many foods that we buy do not stimulate our system adequately, especially fast-foods that are quick to swallow and require very little chewing.

Not only physical substance nourishes, but also what enters us through our eyes. Our sense of sight is most closely connected to light. One can infer from this that human beings, like the plants, are actually fed by light. We respond to the light that has been transformed once it has been absorbed by the plant or by the animal. Plants and animals that are free in nature have a greater nutritional value than factory-farmed creatures and they also taste much better.

Homemakers spend an appreciable time occupied with food, and realize that the visual aspect is essential. Vegetables, herbs, fruits, and meats possess colour and form that the artist's eye selects with knowledge and skill. A meal can be like a picture and a loaf of bread can become a sculpted form. Cakes and puddings are colourful, the texture and sweetness adding to their nutritional splendour. The very best of cooks will see that the beauty of the food is reflected in the table setting and the cosiness of the room itself. Even though it is possible to eat very well in restaurants, to be able to eat at home with friends is often so much nicer. All the senses are brought into play in a gentle and harmonious symphony so that the company sitting round the table can interact whole-heartedly. Could it be that what makes eating out so attractive is because one need not get up to clear the table, nor wash the dishes? When food is cooked with love, it looks and tastes better and if this is extended to the social atmosphere whilst preparing the food, and afterwards when washing the dishes, then the cook has indeed become an artist in the home! Is it possible to create a bit of fun when doing the dishes? It will make the chore easier to do because one can expect company and need no longer to be left to do it all alone. Children love doing dishes because it is an opportunity to play with soapy water. The possibility to play can be stretched into adulthood if the imagination is allowed free reign!

A home where meals are taken together can teach important social graces very naturally. Encouraging an artistic environment at home implies sifting impressions and modifying them so that what is unsuitable is kept to a minimum and that food for the soul and spirit can be as generously offered as food for the body. In a previous chapter, eating regularly was recommended as a very helpful way of establishing sensitivity for the fluctuation of peaceful and active moments in daily life, but meal times offer many other advantages.

Meal Times

Eating together may be the only time in the day when the house-community meets. These can be moments of pleasure, or stress, depending on how we meet each other. We socialize, we consider each other's needs and we enjoy the food, but what makes these times pleasant is when every one contributes good will and friendly conversation.

The first consideration to a meal is obviously the food itself, how it appears, its smell and taste. The next important point is the planning, so that the small quirks and individual tastes can be met with little or no bother. Setting the table is an enjoyable artistic skill and can be enhanced by using flowers or seasonal things to complete the beauty. To make sure that the meal is eaten in peace, one can see to it that all the crockery and cutlery are set out from the beginning. It can be fun to work this out together with children. For a dinner party, a moment's forethought will help. Half the fun lies in the preparation! The master–artist plans the work before offering it up for admiration and appreciation. This preliminary act is an expression of love and will create the warmth of atmosphere that makes a meal so very delightful.

Most things improve when shared with others and the preparation for the meal is no exception. Children love helping in the kitchen and they usually love setting the table because it satisfies something in their neat and tidy souls. This need not end with adulthood. The hidden artist in us rises if given the opportunity, and added to this is the oddly comfortable feeling of having contributed in some way to the cooking.

Eating round a table need not be kept only for social occasions. Sharing food is the beginning of sharing life and laughter and love. Could the abandonment of meal times be one of the reasons why we feel distant and formal towards strangers? Are we losing the art of conversation and warm tolerance that can be learned around the table? Are we too often in a hurry, or too busy to sit down together? Maybe we are sacrificing precious moments of intimacy. Most people can recall childhood meals of fun and laughter, which seemed to enhance the taste of the food. Sadly, most of us can also remember the times when arguments closed the throat, making swallowing very difficult. One can assume that eating and being nourished are not always synonymous, because the atmosphere has as much to do with our ability to digest as does the actual quality of the food.

Though manners and customs vary from country to country, the fundamental reason for their existence remains the same. They are the basis of consideration and tolerance, which comes to the fore when receiving guests, especially strangers. Being a stranger can be painful, but good manners can smooth the way to making friends. Hospitality is the time-honoured art of making people feel wanted and at home, and it always includes the offer of food. In almost every culture it also includes conversation, comfort and care. The meal time belongs to this realm of hospitality and is the place that establishes a sound social basis. Seen in this light it ceases to be a waste of one's precious time and can become the moment most looked for and appreciated in our busy working lives.

Having young children may be offered as a reason not to have formal meal times because we imagine that they cannot sit still for too long. Though this may be the case, generally small children enjoy a large company of people having a good time over a meal, though they may ask to leave the table before the adults have finished eating. In order to encompass adult and adolescent pleasure in longer meal times with lively conversation, setting aside one meal in the day to be taken in common, and allowing the other two to be more child-orientated, could suit the house-community's social endeavours. Children can learn to play quietly whilst others eat and converse, if they are recognized and respected. They usually respond to consideration by imitating it, thus learning the first steps to good manners and gentle customs.

By understanding all the areas of social life that are covered during a meal, we can see that more than just the need for eating is satisfied. However, offering a threefold nutrition that feeds body, soul and spirit means that homemakers need to work sensitively and with knowledge. We need to know that the senses are stimulated by the ambience we are creating and learn how to recognize them. This will provide great assistance in developing an artistic approach to life. Though five senses are well known to everyone, in fact, with objective observation, twelve specialized human senses can be identified.

The Twelve Senses

Nourishing may begin with the sense of sight, but when we eat, all our senses are engaged. The senses of movement and balance respond to the beauty and order around the table. The sense of hearing, too, has its part to play in connection with conversation and general atmosphere. Hearing is, in fact, very closely connected to the process of nourishing, in particular of the soul. What we hear can be tasteful, and a good piece of music can fill one, giving a feeling of satisfaction and repletion. From these small examples we can see that for homemakers, understanding the senses is essential for nourishing the whole human being.

We know that we have five senses and that they are sight, hearing, taste, smell, and touch. But in fact we have a further seven, and together these twelve senses can be divided into groups, which, for the sake of clarity, can be called the lower, the middle, and the higher senses.

The lower senses are *touch, life, movement* and *balance*. The sense of touch is easy to understand. It informs us of the material world, but what is more important to the homemaker is that this sense tells us where the self ends and someone or something else begins. It is the sense of touch that makes us relate sensitively to each other's space, and to the need for our own. It also allows us to know ourselves to be separate from our environment. When touching something, we experience our personal boundary and so know our place in the world.

The sense of life is the feeling of well-being that we tend to notice only when something is wrong. As long as this sense remains unconscious, then we are well and healthy. The sense of life tells us when we feel at home, and makes us aware of feeling secure, both physically and socially. People can be quite ill with homesickness, or from fear of something, which demonstrates the refinement of the sense of life.

The sense of movement gives us mobility and the ability to perceive and place objects and ourselves in space. It allows us to perform chores, do our work, in fact, every kind of ordinary and extraordinary action. This sense is disturbed or stimulated by disorder and order, and is the reason why we tend to feel restless when living in a mess. We can also feel trapped if we live in too tidy a home.

The last of the lower senses is balance. The fact that we can stand upright is due to our sense of balance. It is this sense that informs us of the harmony of objects in our surroundings. The sense of movement will tell us that the picture hangs crooked, but the sense of balance tells us that the relationship of objects and colours blends well, or contrasts creatively.

In the context of the home, the four lower senses are especially bound up with nourishing the soul because they express artistic inclinations, which we all posses to a degree. They reveal the spirit that moves behind the world and so they are the faithful servants of the homemaker who aspires to becoming an artist, because the aim of every artist is to reveal the truth inherent in the world of matter.

The middle senses are *smell, taste, sight, warmth,* and *hearing.* They are familiar and do not require too much explaining. In connection with the home, they are the senses most busy when nourishing the body. Of course, we use them all the time, but especially when eating, socializing and enjoying life. They give us the means to experience joy, and help us to know what satisfaction is, as well as what may do us harm. Bad food smells awful and tastes rotten! We feel miserable if we are cold, and loud noises hurt the eardrums.

The higher senses are the most difficult to experience consciously because they are the most spiritually active. They are the senses of *word, thought* and *ego,* upon which the certainty and independence of thinking is constructed. The sense of word is that purely human faculty of understanding speech as being different from noise, sound or tone. We are able to distinguish meaning in vocalization because we possess a sense of word. Animals vocalize but do not grasp it with meaning. Because we perceive meaning, we can formulate sentences and language can develop.

Speech and conversation are essential ingredients to any social attempt. Real communication is to grasp the meaning and good will in expressions. The sense of word assists us in comprehending the intentions of body language and gesture, as well as in the spoken word, and so a feeling of freedom and self-expression become truly valid qualities within the home.

The sense of thought emerges from the sense of word. This, too, is a uniquely human faculty. It is the gift of understanding the thoughts of others, of being able to follow a trend of thought. Within the home, this is absolutely essential. To become sensitive and responsive to one's house-community is the spiritual way to achieve quality of life.

The sense of ego is the last and highest sense. It is the ability to recognize another person as being human. To experience our own self, we need another person who reflects us. To experience someone else, we need our sense of ego. This is the sense that makes us treat each person as unique. It allows us to develop loyalty, commitment, responsibility, and love. These last three senses are in constant activity, especially when difficulties arise in the home. They make us able to deal with human differences, and keep us alert to the truths of existence.

Recognition of the twelve senses and how they work helps in the task of nurturing a social home life. They convey what is good, beautiful and true, and warn us of the dangers in life. Without the twelve senses we could not absorb the nourishment available to the soul and spirit. The senses work all the time, whether we sleep or are awake and, like windows, they let perceptions flow in and out continually. We imagine, incorrectly, that we close down our senses when we sleep. In fact, we only remove our consciousness from them, which is why people still react to sensory stimulation when anaesthetized, or in a coma.

Young and growing children need most particularly to be surrounded by harmonious and artistic experiences. They usually have a great desire to learn and are open to new and exciting adventures. As we know, they have a zest for living that can appear to be limitless. But just because their senses are so sharp, they can be overwhelmed with impressions and this will reflect in the quality of memory later on in life. Experiences that cannot be digested properly can cause an obstruction in the soul. Patterns of obsessive behaviour may be the result of sensory impact that was too startling or damaging at a vulnerable and tender age. The home that nourishes the whole human being can promote a healthily balanced life of soul.

Nourishing the Soul

What feeds the soul is beauty. In this context, one might imagine that the sense of sight is the most involved, but if one is observant, one can see that actually the four lower senses work just as hard. Art requires and uses all the senses. Within the home, the art of interior decorating is no exception. On entering a room one will respond to its colour and objects in the same way as one does to a work of art.

Decorating need not be equated with huge cost because we usually furnish our homes with familiar and much loved articles as well as new and elegant items. Things that are loved and cherished make our lives comfortable and secure. The new and sparkling addition lights up the quality of life. Homemakers use this rule of thumb when arranging furniture and objects of beauty. Sight, movement, balance and touch all come into play. A picture may look quite wrong on one wall and right on another.

Just as great painters of old employed the assistance of others to finish huge murals, so too can the homemaker involve the house-community in creating an artistic home. This will ease the burden of the housework, because the home becomes a personal expression of those living in it. Tidying and cleaning can be shared since our own creativity is something most of us take pride in and want to see maintained. Dusting and keeping the place in order take on a new value. Wanting to touch and stroke things is a natural instinct to the artist, and so are the loving finishing touches that homemakers like to give. In contrast, it is equally satisfying to stand still and admire a room that one has made beautiful.

In order to create beauty in the home, one enters into a relationship with the inner quality of things. The choice of colour and objects displayed can reflect this, especially in places such as kitchens, laundry, or bathrooms. Here mechanical gadgets and chemical substances enter the picture. They are often not very aesthetically beautiful. Their value lies in their function, but if they are placed in the room where one can use them most efficiently, then they become objects of beauty in their own right. If the backdrop of colour relates to the function of the workplace, then a feeling of satisfaction arises when one works in these spaces. Most homes, like all workshops, have their mechanical aids, which can be compared to the craftsman's basic tools of the trade. They perform the hard and rough groundwork, but they cannot replace the sensitive touch of the human hand. In the home, housework may have become like poor Cinderella, but it can be transformed into its true value as the Princess of all gestures of love. Objects, plants, and animals too, shine when the hand has given its blessing!

It is the voice of Ahriman that encourages us into having as many labour saving devices as we can afford, and Lucifer adds, in his persuasive tone, that this will give us time to do the things we really want to do! Without doubt, household machines are very useful and necessary. But they often make a great deal of noise. This affects the senses, and stimulates the nerves, which causes hidden tiredness and may be the actual source of the irritation we feel when using these efficient machines. They drain our nervous energy, so it is helpful to think about this side effect when using them in our daily life. We keep the material world and the influences of Ahriman and Lucifer in their proper places by working with the gift of conscious thought that resides in the soul.

To nourish us so that we can use our consciousness with warmth and spiritual insight, we reach into the world of nature for its intrinsic beauty. For this reason, an aspect of the home lies with the world of plants and animals, but it will always be a matter of personal taste whether nature actually enters the house itself. Animals and plants will, of course, be present in the garden, but since many homes cannot enjoy this luxury, these kingdoms do find their way into the home or apartment. It is natural to enjoy contact with nature, and animals that are loved and cared for bring richness and fun as well as teaching respect for living things. Growing and caring for house plants or window boxes brings light and colour and scent into the home. It is a moment in the day when the homemaker can do something slowly and meditatively, for no other particular reason than to create beauty. To do something of this kind opens up a small space in one's very busy daily life and can act as a restorative to hungry souls.

Nourishing the Soul with Nature and Culture

Beauty can be found everywhere. The view of hill or valley fills us with pleasure and our eyes drink in the wonders. Many people long to live close to nature because its beauty is unforced and free. Some have a favourite place where, in moments of suffering or joy, the soothing flow of the landscape can help to balance the extremes of emotion. However, the expression of beauty in our civilized inheritance is very different. What the human being can design, build, paint or portray in so many artistic ways stimulates our senses by awakening thought. To the homemaker, nature and culture can be resourced from the wider environment, and perhaps also reflected in the home at festive moments.

Children obtain great satisfaction from exploring both the new and the old, and love outings, whether it means going out in the country or into the city. The enthralling objects in a museum, or the magic in the theatre, or the first visit to an old country manor and park, are exciting experiences. They are equally precious to adults who can enjoy with new freshness the marvels of human creativity through the pleasure of their children. Learning to respect nature at an early age lasts the whole of one's life. For example, delighting in picking flowers can be enhanced if one learns to do this so that some will remain for the next time. This will help to prevent the general adolescent tendency to want to dominate one's environment, an inclination that usually passes as one gains confidence within one's new boundaries of experience. Vandalism is a lack of understanding of the living being of Mother Nature. The vandalism that arises towards man-made objects comes from a lack of opportunity in early childhood to learn about the wonders of human inventiveness, and the marvellous skills that we can learn from watching our parents go about their daily work. To enjoy natural or cultural things may mean to select appropriately age-related events, but to witness the childish awe that children show at the wonders of life is as nourishing for the soul of the homemaker, as going to the concert of one's choice. However, this too is necessary, because to nourish, one must also be nourished!

Cultural activities can be carried out at home, too. When seeking ways to celebrate traditional festivals, it is fun to get together and write a new play where there can be a role for every one in the house-community. It is surprising what dramatic talents can lie in people, and how much one can enjoy theatre in one's sitting-room! A dramatic production involves all kinds of off as well as on stage aspects and needs.

There are the costumes to be made, the set to paint, and someone will need to make the musical sound effects. Given the right mood, all can enjoy themselves in the creativity. Staging plays may happen more easily in homes where there are children who love to dress up and role play. Adult house-communities may choose rather to read poetry together, or play music. The fun and nourishment comes from the attempt and the social interaction, rather than the perfection of the outcome. Biscuits, cakes, drinks, and good company revolve around what may turn into a very touching, beautiful or possibly hilarious production. Laughter is not only a medicine, it also feeds! Simplicity is the key, and then culture can link hearts. Inviting friends and neighbours to participate will create a small society, because doing things together is food for lonely souls.

Connecting to one's neighbourhood can also be through cultivating the environment around one's house. A garden that is cared for and full of flowers, or where there is space in which to play hide-and-seek, or a lawn on which one can sit and enjoy the sun, is a pleasure to see for those who live round about. There is nothing more lovely when walking in the city, or out in the country, than to come across well tended gardens. It is as though the love in the home has spilled over into the road or street for every passer-by to bathe in for a little moment. We are very much more influenced by our environment than we consciously recognize! Social science points to the influences that parenting, or the lack of it, has on growing children. It is equally important to realize that what surrounds us physically has as much effect on us as what envelops us by way of human relationships, when one is attempting to nurture a home life that can help us to live creatively in society.

Malnutrition of the Soul

Human beings are basically social and everywhere in the world one can see evidence of this fact in the existence of large cities, towns and little villages. We do not, as a rule, live in completely isolated conditions. The consequences of this tendency can be very advantageous, in that we can help each other and learn from each other. But there are unfortunate disadvantages too. Because of the centralizing of peoples, and our present-day technological inventiveness, sound, light, and air pollution are becoming a serious threat to our health. We worry about the thinning ozone layer. It would be equally relevant to worry about increases in noise and interference in light.

Our senses react to all stimulation, and consequently the body also reacts. Constant sound causes muscle movements, and continuous artificial light plays on the nerves. Because of this physiological activity, we directly affect the quality of our sleep. We actually force ourselves to sleep in spite of noise, and many of us live our lives rarely seeing all the stars in the heavens. This lack of true sleep means that our spiritual companions find it very difficult to converse with us, and we bring little spiritual nourishment back into our waking life.

In many cases these hindrances cannot be avoided. We need to make a home where we can also earn a living. But there are some things over which we *do* have control and they need not invade the home that aims to become socially sound and creative. The world around us encompasses many useful technological inventions such as the television, the radio, and computer technology, but these bring in their wake an unfortunate potential for dulling imaginative inventiveness. Though they are very useful in their place, we have the tendency to let them become too influential in our daily life, as well as our cultural and educational efforts.

The problem with these machines is that firstly, they make a constant noise, be it ever so slight, and that secondly, they utilize neon lighting, a form of illumination that has a very slight, continuous flicker. These activities stimulate the senses, which, as we know, cannot shut down as long as they are in working order. From a very early age, we learn to tune-out and block out the impressions coming from these machines. Just as we no longer hear cars passing when we live on a busy stretch of road, we no longer notice the television, or the background music of the radio. But the senses notice, and pressure is put on the nerves to expend yet more energy.

It is not uncommon to find background radio at meal times, and the TV dinner is widely advertised as a great source of relaxation! We ignore the slight movements that the flickering screen incites in our muscles, and we close off from registering the music that our ears hear. In fact, we are eating, drinking, digesting, hearing, seeing, moving, balancing, and shutting them all out of our consciousness, all at the same time. We are, on such occasions, in grave danger of becoming utterly hyperactive!

The sense of hearing, which is perhaps the most exhausted by these technological inventions, is one of the finest contributors to our ability to live together in harmony. We really need to *talk to, and listen to* each other in order to understand each other! Unlike the animals, we can switch off our consciousness from whatever disturbs us, but to do so we need to use our nervous energy. This creates tension because the nervous system is very finely tuned to needs of the senses and can get over stimulated. This is another generator of irritability, like static electricity, and can lead to a selfish lack of consideration for others, the root of which may be in a very necessary desire to be able to relax from outer demands. Indiscriminate use of technology can cause unspecified exhaustion. It is even possible that a portion of the restless behaviour as well as the low boredom threshold of teenagers may stem from too great an exposure to stimulation of this kind.

The popularity of loud disco music can unfortunately damage our delicate hearing mechanism. The fact that the walkman requires the use of earphones that are frequently tuned to a high volume will not help our fine auditory nerves. The mobile phone is suspected to be a contributor to cancer. We are warned of the dangers to health and safety in relation to these artefacts, but the risk to a healthy social life is perhaps just as great. Every age has made wonderful new scientific discoveries, and every age has cried out: 'Heresy!' and consequently learnt to live with, and even become dependent upon technological advances. But in every age, too, the artist, actor, poet and musician have taken an equally valid place side by side with the modern inventions.

With the advent of our highly mechanized society, are we running the risk of relegating the human artistic skills of the imagination to second place behind the great leaps that our intellect is taking? Do we still value the creative skills alive in crafts and manual work? Computers in primary schools may be advantageous to ease technological know-how, though one can question whether children will not acquire computer literacy just as effectively a little later on in life. Perhaps, if as much emphasis were placed on acquiring imaginative and artistic manual skills at an early age, we would succeed in balancing the wonders of science with the spiritual insights that art can give to us.

Fortunately, within the home, such choices can be freely made. One can decide how much television and video games are played in a day. One can limit the use of the computer, or even choose not to have one. One need not have background music, and one can ask that radio decibel levels are kept reasonable. One can discourage the walkman and mobile telephone. In homes that include young children, technology of this kind is not really necessary and may even be harmful to their tender and lively senses.

A reasonable approach to what might be problems of culture and conscience by means of conversation based on interest in each other's needs will usually meet with good results. Most people are very open to discussion, and usually have a sound idea of what is healthy, and what creates a social environment. If these choices are made on the grounds of understanding the debilitating effect of technology where nurturing the strengths and creative potential is the aim, one will reach a fair conclusion.

If one examines the uses and advantages that modern technology has given us, one can wonder why they should be so harmful to human development. Have they not been invented to help us? Why do we find that some children become less imaginative and playful? Why do adolescents, who seem to have become so clever, often appear to be so careless in social endeavours? How can perfectly rational adults become couch-potatoes or computer addicts?

The influence of machinery can be seen from a point of view other than its efficiency, if one looks to the source of its power. Almost everything in our life utilizes the same form of energy. All our comforts, our global awareness, our ability to travel round the world and most of our products are at some time or another dependent upon electricity, a portion of which comes from nuclear reactors. Electricity originates from decaying light particles, so we are, in fact, dependent upon dead light. If we remember how human beings, animals and plants feed on light, then we realize that we are ingesting, through our senses, an enormous amount of decaying light, of dead food.

Our nervous system is the only part of us that can absorb this and utilize it. Therefore the intellect, which works through our nerves and brain cells, is becoming more and more acute, but at the cost of the imagination, which feeds on living light only. We need our imagination because it can deal with the realities of human endeavour by means of its spiritual flexibility, which the intellect, with its perfect logic, cannot achieve. Homemakers know that we do not only use our intellect when relating to other people. With logic one can go straight to the point, but with imagination one can experience compassion and understanding. The intellect certainly needs stimulating, as does the imagination, but if they are healthily balanced, then information technology and transmitted entertainment will fall into their rightful places. A home without television, computer and radio may be serene, artistic, and filled with culture, but the technology of today need not destroy this, if it is used with common sense.

Adolescents are highly attracted to technology. Unfortunately they have not yet fully acquired an independent sense of self, and though they have left the imaginative play of childhood behind, they have not yet developed mature judgement. At this age in life we are most at risk to the wiles of Lucifer and Ahriman, though it would be a mistake to think that we are not always in danger of succumbing to their influence. However, the teenager can be fed with any amount of mediocre, even downright evil thoughts and pictures via the media. The indigestion that follows often shows up in stylized and patterned thoughts, language and behaviour. Young children, too, are very vulnerable, especially to televised images, which they experience as real, much to Ahriman's delight.

Lucifer employs different means. He offers culture filled with violence, melodrama and sexuality that extend the frontiers of excitement, feeding it to us by means of media entertainment. When young people appear to be tired, moody and yet seek entertainment for which they need offer no creative actions, then Lucifer rejoices at his success in cheating humanity of nourishing life forces.

Contrary to what one is led to believe, homes with no television are attractive to children because they can play without distraction and use their very fertile imagination. Homes where discriminating use of technology is the norm attract adolescents because they can find people willing to discuss, and to listen. Homes where information technology and televised entertainment are utilized for business purposes and occasional interests are attractive to adults because here one can find a real potential for relaxation and restoration of heart and mind. Homemakers have the possibility to nurture a social environment in which such potential can find fulfilment.

Fundamental Food for the Soul

Surprising though it may seem, what is most nourishing for the soul is to work with our hands. To design and build up our surroundings is extremely satisfying because we love to feel that where we live reflects the best of our personality. When presented with the challenge of making a home with objects and in circumstances that may not be ideal, a surge of enthusiasm often arises, followed by a feeling of contentment, especially if the end result comes close to the original aims and intentions. These feelings come about because we are playing our senses like the strings of a harp, but the music is not so much audible, as visible, in the harmony that has been physically created.

We do not, however, only live in the comfortable home that we have made. We also work in it, as all homemakers know! People who share their lives with small children will observe how happy and contented they become when in the presence of adults who are busily at work. They love constructive activities, but seem to enjoy less to be with someone who reads a book or works on a computer. In fact, they often interrupt these activities, not understanding them to be work in the same sense as working with the hands. They especially love to help with housework, re-enacting experiences in the much-favoured game of

'Mummies and Daddies'. They learn about life whilst playing these games, as well as about their cultural heritage, but no matter what their background, playing at work gives them a satisfied, serious and well-fed air. Sadly, there are children who, for one reason or another, have not had the advantage of experiencing a home in which these games can be played. They tend to express their inner loss by destructive or even aggressive actions towards their environment.

Play is no longer the same for the adolescent. At this time in life, enjoyment comes more from being part of social projects and they can be very inventive at finding new ways to alleviate the lot of the less fortunate. It fills their growing souls with immense satisfaction. Young people whose homes may not have featured social activities may be precisely those who need the challenge of creative acts. The so-called delinquent, when offered the opportunity to work with hands and muscles, often proves to be an artist of design and colour.

Generally, using one's hands skilfully satisfies everyone, no matter what the age. People who work in businesses that depend upon intellectual and mental capacities, frequently have surprisingly practical hobbies, which they enjoy doing at home. The contrast this gives to their daily duties is experienced as refreshing and nourishing. But enjoying one's work can be just as fulfilling, especially if one is fortunate enough to have a job that has an artistic aspect to it. And most household chores, though physically quite demanding, have the qualifying advantage of involving intellectual capacities, as well as creative skills. The variety of tasks within the home means that within a working week administration, finances, education, counselling, nutrition, nursing, horticulture, craftwork and decorating all appear. The social skills of homemaking can weave all these aspects together into a wholesome life style. Most homemakers will know the feeling of warm satisfaction that rises up after a good week's work well done.

Meaningful work comes from a deeply spiritual source, and the desire to be positively engaged in it is born in us. We bring this purpose with us as a formative part of our karma, which we have gained from our previous incarnation.

The Karmic Meaning of Sense Impressions

As we have already discovered, sleeping and waking are a comparison in our everyday life that corresponds to the great cosmic act of dying and being born again. When we sleep and converse with the angels, we are linking in to a cyclic process, but with less vastness of intention. We are merely preparing ourselves for the next day. This means that we wake up again, remembering what happened yesterday, but with the added dimension of having just had a refreshing night's sleep. We take yesterday's acts, thoughts, intentions and feelings into the new day, hopefully with a better and more constructive colouring than the day before. If the previous day's happenings have been on the negative side, we may wake with a burdened conscience and the feeling of wanting to redress the balance. If our memory is of cheerful and successful things, we go forward into the day with enthusiasm and positivity. But we never consider that yesterday's events can have no bearing on today's. We know that all our deeds have consequences and so act accordingly in every new day.

We know that the absolute certainty of memory, and knowledge of consequences, is the basis for trust in the order of life. Having no memory is painfully disconcerting and prevents one from acting coherently, or with meaning. Trust is the foundation of the feeling of being at home in our body, and in the world. Since home is the place where we sleep, then home becomes the very centre of our existence on earth. It is here that our potential can unfold because of the sound and unquestioning confidence that can be built within it.

The task of homemaking is therefore a very spiritual one. It encompasses protection of sensory impressions in a way that can allow every one a sound and healthy sleep at the end of a day. Sleep is sometimes referred to as *the little brother of death*. Knowledge of the connection that the senses have to life after death takes on new importance for the home-maker, once it is grasped how much of what is experienced at home influences the karma of this life and of the next.

The twelve senses can be compared to twelve windows of the soul. They each have their designated place in the body, though none are open in the brain. This large organ acts only as a synthesizer, gathering up what rises from within the life body as memories in order to reflect them to our consciousness. The brain can be described as a *mirror* that reflects everything. These reflections are stored in the living muscles, not in the brain! This can be grasped by observing how we act in life. Usually we learn by *doing*, and remember best when we have performed the necessary actions. We do many things without thinking about them, because our hands and body seem to remember the movements, like driving a car, swimming, or riding a bicycle. Almost all skills, even the academic ones, are acquired through practice rather than theory. We become conscious of our memory only once our thinking draws it up into the brain.

Our brain, however, is an impartial reflector, and so it also mirrors the intentions of angels that reach down to us through the power of thought. This explains why we can wake up with new ideas that we sense to be inspirations. These experiences delight poets and inventors because they feel addressed by their Muse. We know now that every human being can be blessed in this way, receiving the spiritual reflections that enter our power of thinking in the form of ideals, inspiration and truth, which sink down into our soul. We experience the rich memories of how we have carried out our deeds, and the angels take these in as food given by humanity. We, in turn, experience as nourishment the spiritual insights that the angels offer to us.

In this way we can recognize two complementary streams of nourishment that flow from humanity to the cosmos and from the cosmos to humanity. We can see that it really *does* matter that sense impressions within the home be as healthy and true as possible. When we use our limbs creatively, and in particular our hands, we express what we feel to be spiritually true on the earth. The angels can read this script, and so can feed us with true spiritual imaginations in return.

When we die, we offer all that was true in life to the spiritual world, but to be born again, we need to equip ourselves for life on earth. We know how to build our new identity, soul, and abilities, because in our previous incarnation our senses had learnt about the world.

This is a staggering thought! What we do with our hands today has the potential to dictate the quality and perspective of our thoughts in a life to come. What we do as moral deeds, what we think as clear intentions, and with what we surround ourselves in our daily lives, will have their consequences on the karma of this life *and the next*. It is this innate knowledge that steers us to want to work with our hands, to want to create beauty, order and art in our lives. The homemaker who understands this fundamental truth of existence will encourage desire for healthy sensory impressions. The home that nurtures work, creativity and the intellect in fair measure can lay the foundation for an understanding of all that the earth and the cosmos can offer towards human development.

Nourishing the Spirit

Whenever a truth comes to light, a certain inner tranquillity arises. One has a sense of recognition, of familiarity, which gives immense satisfaction. This feeling comes into being because the ego, which is unique and spiritual in every human being, is nourished. Virtues such as honesty, conscience and morality, feed the spirit and these qualities must be nourished in order not to wither and die.

The hindrances that Ahriman and Lucifer cast in the path of development take on very subtle forms when it comes to deep spiritual truths. They offer us condonement, instead of tolerance, and a careless live-and-let-live approach, instead of compassionate involvement in humanity's struggle for insight. They make us confuse integrity with prejudice, and moral choices with discrimination.

Children are sometimes much wiser than adults, because they see soul and spirit truths in the wisdom of fairy-tales. They experience the princes and princesses, witches and dragons, as images of the eternal struggle between light and darkness, between truth and falsehood. They appreciate the absolute justice of the blood-thirsty endings, not because they are monsters but because they still see the truth uncovered and that moral goodness will always win in the end. The imagination of the story-teller allows the listeners to form their own images and so be fed by the spirit.

One of the most rewarding and pleasurable sides to homemaking is to be the story-teller, or reader, and where there are children, there will always be a place for fairy-tales and other stories. Many impressions throughout the day can make a hard impact, and though they may not be as ugly, witnessed cruelty in life is always a shocking experience. To tell a home-made fairy-tale that portrays these events imaginatively can put such happenings into perspective, and bring back truth into children's lives. Love can be taught to the young listener by means of images that heal the hurts of existence without moralizing. Literature and poetry are the outcome of human attempts to find and express truth. Homes where story telling and books are as precious as plants, animals and art, are places where the human spirit can find nourishment.

Homemakers can be called upon to deal with crises, and it is not uncommon in such moments to feel quite helpless and ignorant. It is also not uncommon suddenly to find words or gestures that alleviate the stress of the moment. From where did such wisdom arise and how did one suddenly become a channel for it? There are spiritual qualities available to the homemaker that can be used in daily life, and devotion is one such tool. When in distress, the human being prays, not perhaps so much in words, but more by opening up a *devotional space* in the soul into which spiritual activity can pour. Consciously cultivating devotion in daily life means that one learns to open the soul voluntarily to spiritual guidance. On a more practical level, in order to devote oneself to a job or activity, one must give it the benefit of one's complete attention and concentration. By doing this one usually learns something new about it, one remembers how to do it and one learns to do it perfectly. In this way the spirit in matter can become accessible. Devotion means prayer as well as practical deeds. When we pray, we devote ourselves to the spiritual world and ask for intercession in a world that may need a little help. Devotion to the practical deeds of life means to pray in daily life.

Usually we forget this because Ahriman does not wish us to remember that the spirit can be of practical use. He slips scepticism into the tired homemaker and Lucifer takes advantage of the moment to add a feeling of disbelief. Then the one follows on from the other, whispering that daily life is not the place in which to develop real spiritual potential, and that devotion is anyway only a religious experience! Devoting oneself to a task does not mean that it needs to become more complex and that one must lose one's sense of humour! On the contrary, it will probably become easier because one will learn how to carry it out, and understand its true nature more clearly. This cannot fail to give a delightful sense of fulfilment.

Nourishing the Homemaker

To become an artist in one's chosen field is a lifetime's work, but the effort to achieve this ambition is worth every moment. It is nourishment in itself, because it lends purpose and credibility to one's striving. Reverence, devotion and wonder are tools for the soul of the artist. The homemaker too, uses these tools in daily life, in order to create beauty, truth and goodness with which every home can be filled. Ahriman and Lucifer will always try to make us think that homemaking is unprofessional and out-dated, or fit only for simple souls. But the home is the foundation for all spiritual endeavours because it is the place where reverence, devotion and wonder can be nurtured. It is from home that we go out into the world, bringing these spiritual qualities to our environment.

To devote oneself to building a home where warmth, light, love and laughter are to be experienced cannot fail to make a difference to life in general. Recognizing that one can heal the rootless feeling of anxiety is to know that one is performing a spiritually valid task. What was meaningless has become as clear as crystal and as light as the spirit.

5

Meeting the Needs

Secreting

Wherever we work, live or play we find ourselves having to meet needs of one kind or another. In order to meet expectations with some efficiency and good humour it is very helpful to keep up one's inner balance. But moments may arise when one's equilibrium is disturbed. It may be that the small, unnoticed changes in one's body upset the balance and we experience this as a change of mood or feeling. This happens to both men and women, for example, when falling in love. We react physically to the changing relationship and immediately our outlooks, feelings and desires take on a new direction. The changes can work both ways, sparked off by glandular activity or by outer events that stimulate the glands, for example, when something frightens us. Our kidneys respond with a rush of adrenaline and we find the strength to act with extra energy in order to meet the danger. This shows how the soul affects the body and the body affects the soul, and in this reciprocal way we are able to meet nature's demands.

The most commonplace illustration of this activity relates to eating. We secrete the appropriate saliva in order that the food can be digested. We have to break it down so that it can be absorbed. The glands in the mouth begin this process of secreting chemicals at the very moment when we think of the food that we are going to eat. Hunger causes saliva to flow. The miracle of this life process is that the secretions produced will always exactly meet the requirements that will most successfully break down the food. As the food moves further down from the mouth into the digestive tract and into the stomach, the chemicals change until it is so thoroughly altered that the etheric life-giving forces can be extracted from the physical matter. These forces are absorbed into the body in order to maintain our life and strength. The rest is expelled from the body by means of the process of excretion.

The life process that includes the magic of secretion and the miracle of excretion can be called the process of *secreting*. The balancing activity of the glandular and lymph system helps the human body to deal with the influences and substances that enter it from outside. Therefore it is through their work that we maintain the immune system that is our life body, the etheric protection that keeps us intact. The immune system allows the human being to remain healthy by being a buffer between outer and inner physical needs.

If our immune system is weakened or does not function very well then poisons can enter the body. Much of what we take in as food, drink, and medicine is potentially deadly, but because of the remarkably adept and transformative ability of the body to secrete the right substances, those elements that could do us harm are transformed and what we cannot use is processed and discarded. A healthy glandular system is the basis for balance of the body and equanimity within the soul. For example, an imbalance of the thyroid gland can make life either very intense or very slow and depressing. In such cases, only medicines can help to stabilize this condition. Swings of mood caused by glandular disorders, upsetting the balance and making it difficult to find the right reaction to life, are one aspect. But there are also the small ups and downs that minimal hormonal changes may create in the people with whom we share our lives, and they touch us just as intimately. Mood swings happen to everyone and they have an effect on everyone around. In order to deal with them, we try to acquire patience and a degree of social skills.

Recognizing the link between glandular changes and

mood swings can be a great help to the homemaker who is faced with meeting the needs of daily life. When someone's hormones are not in balance then the potential for hysteria and unreasonable behaviour is so much greater. A doctor might have recourse to medicines in order to deal with such events, but the homemaker usually has to find some other means of meeting such challenges. Developing flexibility and balance within daily life requires a depth of understanding of human frailties and human potential, as well as an acceptance of one's own limitations.

Meeting Needs in Daily Life

Homemaking concerns people and one can never really know what might happen in a person's life. An exciting, but also challenging aspect of homemaking is that sticking to a plan without considering the unexpected is rarely possible. One has to learn to take each day at a time and be prepared for any eventuality. One is constantly assessing and reassessing situations. To be alert to the needs is a great asset because then the potential for answering them can become an actual skill.

There are two ways of coping with a life style based on the unknown. In the first instance one can decide to ignore irrelevancies and stick to one's plans, forcing the circumstances to suit one's prejudgements. This can be a very efficient and effective way of dealing with the unexpected, but it has the tendency to lack heart and soul. In the second place one can let surprises dominate the day, moving loosely from what was planned to the newly arising tasks. This is a friendly and lively method of coping but it has the tendency to lack decisiveness.

The eventual breakdown of both systems is very probable. The destruction of the first lies in the fact that at home one cannot rigidly hold to a plan. Human beings are prone to accidents, to mistakes, and to desperate and immediate needs. To ignore a plea for assistance because it does not fit into one's plans is not necessarily always helpful. The second method tends to lead to an inner and outer chaos. To be at everyone's beck and call is unhealthy and stressful. This can culminate in the absurdity of not knowing what to do about anything!

To find a balanced approach to life asks one to observe the facts of the actual happening. As we already know, our senses absorb everything around us. When we take note of what we are experiencing, then we will be able to sensitize our consciousness so that the power of observation can transform itself into insight. Very often things are not quite what the superficial encounter would have us believe. For example, the child who develops odd secretive habits such as hiding a holy book under the pillow, or arranging toys precisely, and in a certain order, is displaying inclinations that mean something. These strange new habits may merely signify fear of sleep because of bad dreams. Maybe they mean that obsessions are beginning to form because of something that the child cannot properly handle in school or in daily life. Perhaps it may even be the signs of a more serious disability, which is only now coming to the surface. Many things that happen at home are of deep significance. If this is taken seriously, the more troublesome events will begin to offer their own answers because an exact and fine observation has brought them to our awareness.

Observing changes in the body can indicate something of importance just as clearly as changes in habits. Skin tone can tell us so much about what is happening inside another person. If the normal quality and colour alters, this could indicate the onset of illness, or it could indicate a deep-seated anxiety. It could also mean that something very significant has happened and the individual cannot yet find a way to talk about it. Changes in the level of perspiration are equally important to note, particularly in children and adolescents. If the soul is in retreat, or cannot deal with life, then this may show in changes of the natural buoyancy of the hair. Hair is the first indicator of a change in the sweat glands. It is common knowledge to appreciate the changes in perspiration due to fear, shock, or other stressful emotions, but these sensitive glands also respond and alter to minute changes of balance in the soul.

Children react immediately to emotional stimulation by changing the appearance of the skin. Adolescents suffer from general major hormonal changes, so that the appearance of the skin cannot always be relied on as a measure of their inner stability. However, one can develop the sensitivity to notice whether these differences are triggered by the soul, or by the hormones themselves. Distinguishing which comes first can help in finding the most helpful responses. The ability to make these fine distinctions requires an acknowledgement of the fact that individuals adapt differently to situations and events. This varies according to the natural temperaments with which we are born.

The Four Basic Temperaments

Everyone has a basic outlook on life that seems to be influenced by his or her very own unique individuality. Yet, if one examines humanity with observant objectivity, there are actually only four different dispositions with which to work in life.

There are the people who react very quickly and decisively to everything. They hold strong opinions and are not in the least bit shy to state them. Childhood in general sees the world in this positive light, though individuals may belong specifically to this particular outlook. They are the boisterous, confident, loud children who have no trouble breaking the ice in a new relationship, but they can be somewhat domineering to their peers. Adults who fit into this group are often high achievers with very definite targets towards which they work. They can be called *choleric* by nature.

A second group are those who tend to take life very seriously, worry quite a bit, and generally expect the worst. They are often the actors and artists who are able through their very sensitive souls to understand what lies behind human behaviour. In children, the tendency to worry can be very marked, which manifests in a shy and rather sensitive way of relating to their peers. Such children are often a little gloomy in their reactions and thoughts and are therefore easily affected by the opinions of others, approaching life with a *melancholic* air.

A third group are the pretty, light and colourful people who move effortlessly from one situation to another, sometimes cheerful, sometimes sad, but always quick to recover from any event. The *sanguine* being portrays the very essence of childhood, most children being light and sunny by nature, both quick to interest and quick to forget. However, some people retain this quality all through their lives.

The fourth group are the steady, reliable, and quiet people, slow to start and slightly stubborn once they have really got themselves going. Not many children see life in this way, and their quicker companions may tease those that do. Such children often grow up to become rocks of reliability in adulthood, but the peaks and troughs of a more versatile outlook rarely touch them. An underlying *phlegmatic* outlook governs their disposition.

These four types of people tend to deal with life's ups and downs according to their own particular approach, which they seem to bring with them from birth. The flexibility and balance that the homemaker can offer from the standpoint of accurate observation of these groupings can smooth the hazardous yet exciting path of emotions. Many people struggle to find equanimity, particularly if their individual nature is strongly coloured by their physical constitution. It is very different to be born assertive and temperamental than filled with pessimism and melancholia. To be delightfully spontaneous and therefore easily forgiving of slights will make life very different than if one plods along reliably and steadily on the course one has systematically set out for oneself.

These fundamental possibilities of outlook are known as the four temperaments, that is: the *choleric, melancholic, sanguine*, and *phlegmatic*. They set the scene for our reaction to inner and outer events. They colour our moods, as well as our souls, and show up in the manner in which we deal with our daily lives. Because they are the basis of our physical constitution we cannot change them radically, but we can learn to balance ourselves within them, so that the one does not dominate more than another does. Children have to learn this. Adolescents seem to struggle so hard for balance that the temperament can sometimes be an actual support for survival. Adults can begin to work at developing their temperament so that they may acquire a little of those of which they have the least.

To the homemaker, assessing the most active temperament of everyone in the home can be very helpful when having to deal with the unexpected. The response will alter depending on who has delivered the surprise! For instance, reacting to a choleric outburst with melancholic despair is not always the wisest thing to do. Sometimes a calm, phlegmatic reassurance is a much better way of putting out the potential conflagration. Should a crisis arise for the melancholic, who finds life hard to face at the best of times, then a cheerful, joking answer may not be the most tactful assistance. Perhaps a serious proposal offered as a challenge can help to relight the fires of enthusiasm. A quickly flung insult from the sanguine person should probably simply be ignored because that person will have forgotten it immediately. But neglecting his or her sensitive soul can cause deep unhappiness. To try to smooth this over by continuing on regardless will probably have less effect than voicing the hurts that have been inflicted and subsequently accepting the heart-felt apologies. In this way, working with the temperaments can be an invaluable strength for the homemaker.

The silent cries for support, as well as the louder ones, are all part of daily life, and all of them are best met by a quality of flexibility both in mood and deed. Sometimes dropping a plan in order to give full attention to a situation is the wisest thing to do. At other times, carrying on quietly but with an open heart and ear, will help in the task of homemaking. There may even be times when ignoring the demand yet at the same time silently supporting the person's need might be the most positive way of dealing with an event.

To act spontaneously as well as appropriately requires inner resources as well as recognition of general human frailties. To do this the homemaker, too, needs support and sustenance so that adaptability does not turn into impulsiveness and restlessness. A warm and loving observation of moods can consolidate the realities that we face every day. As has already been expressed, an interest in each person's life provides the background as well as a constant source of inspiration. But unless we accept that what we notice is relevant, right into the tiniest detail, we may miss early warning signals and so be faced with situations to which there may appear to be no answer. Minute changes in basic functions of the body's processes are often the key, and the place where these alterations come to light is in the bathroom. Here we take off our clothes and so also our outer protective persona.

The Bathroom

The bathroom is a wonderful place! This is where we take our bodies seriously. And because we are sensitive, and our bodies are precious to us, we tend to want to protect ourselves and so we keep them rather secret from the world. Human beings have only a thin layer of skin with which to cover themselves, whereas animals have furry pelts, or colourful feathers, or scaly skins inside which they can hide. They feel neither shame nor fear about their outer appearance. But the human being in our present day usually feels that to be naked by decision is a great deal more bearable than to feel exposed without preparation. Generally, we tend to feel a degree of embarrassment, almost shame, if we are surprised without our clothes.

Perhaps this is the reason why we usually like to keep the place where we wash a private and protected room. The bathroom is the place where we disrobe and so it is quite natural to want privacy for these moments in the day. It is also the place where we relieve ourselves of the substances that we do not need. This too we prefer to do in secret. For many people, the bathroom is the place where one can relax and let go of masks, pretences, pressure and stressful things. For parents it may often be the only time when they can be really alone! Then the bathroom takes on an aura of sanctuary. There are even some people who run to the bathroom when deeply hurt, or moved, or afraid. Locking the door can provide a feeling of being in a haven. One can block out the world.

The things that constitute a bathroom are objects of hygiene, and their primary aim is to facilitate freshness and also presentation. We *assemble* ourselves in the bathroom. We clean, groom and cherish our outer appearance. To be able to do this whilst gathering up our peace of mind means that the bathroom needs to be warm, clean and inviting. If there are plants, books, magazines and pictures, it can be a delightful as well as cosy place, and the utilitarian mirrors, seats, water and soaps become a useful part of its beauty. Pleasing the senses can offer a level of security. There are some people for whom shedding clothes means to shed the day's cares, which is a pleasant feeling, but there are others who find this an experience of vulnerability. Some children are reluctant to undress because they feel exposed and it almost frightens them. The adolescent love of fashion and make-up is often from a need to transform for visual effect. But for us all, the bathroom offers safety to the sensitive.

To the observant homemaker, the state of bowel and bladder tells a lot about people's nutritional needs, but it also tells a great deal about people's needs of soul. Those who are prone to constipation are often people who suffer from tension. Daily demands make them close up. People who need to relieve themselves constantly tend to be more inclined to anxiety. We all know how often we need to visit the bathroom when we are nervous. And we can sympathize with people who have so much to do that they seem hardly to get the time to go at all!

Then there are those people who spend hours in the bathroom and when they finally come out, they leave a trail of bits and pieces. The mirror, however, clean and shining, has been polished and no condensation can be found on it! The fact that we use mirrors may indicate insecurity in our presentation of the self, but it may equally well mean that our need of self-expression overrides our awareness of the needs of others. Mirrors can be educational because they reflect us as we are. However, we also need them to help us to create who we want to be.

In fact, what the homemaker can learn from this important room in the house is invaluable. Especially where children are concerned, the bathroom is the place where the minute changes that may indicate illness, anxiety, tension, fear, and confidence or growing self-esteem become visible. How children relate to water also shows something about their developing individuality. Most of them love water play, making soap bubbles and messing about. Relaxing in water can provide balance to the conformity that daily life imposes on them. They have to cope with learning how to present themselves within society, but naked in the bath, they can be little slippery charming children, free of inhibitions.

Adolescents usually love bathrooms, appreciating the potential for privacy. They use a great deal of water or none at all, depending on their state of soul. Here too, water equalizes. It washes off the persona and so, for a moment, even the adolescent can look at the unmasked self in safety. The bathroom is the place to *put on one's face* and where one can try out different presentations in search of the self. The drifting smell of perfumes, deodorants and aftershave indicate which personality may be about to emerge! It can be rather trying for the house-community to live with adolescents and their fondness of the bathroom, but to the young person there is no other place so safe nor as securely private.

Adults too, enjoy the privacy and peace of the bathroom, but perhaps they leave less of themselves behind. Nevertheless, homemakers who have learnt the value of observation will notice if someone spends longer than usual at their ablutions, or changes their perfume. Washing off the day's cares, or preparing oneself to meet life can take more or less time, depending on one's feeling of balance and security. We make changes to our appearance in order to cope with moods and tensions, fears and expectations. We also make these changes in order to present our chosen persona. Precisely in those places where the greatest mess is created can the real balances or imbalances be noted. To the homemaker, the bathroom can become a revelation, telling each person's individual story and giving clear indications of individual need, be it physical, social, or spiritual.

Cleanliness at Home

Wherever human beings go things are moved around and changes are made. Moreover, there seems to be an unwritten law that the more people there are, the more mess there seems to be. There even exist those people whom mess seems to follow around! Using things may be the reason for which objects are designed and most things are made to be useful, to be handled and to fulfil necessary functions. But once used, one would hope that they are returned to their rightful place. Human nature being what it is, however, we seem to have to learn to keep things tidy!

In a workshop or office, an expectation for the place to be kept in good working order is sensible, and someone will be employed to clean up. In a library, classroom or surgery this rule will hold good. In hospitals, where hygiene may be a matter of life or death, using things appropriately is very important. But oddly enough, worrying about order at home may not carry the same weight. Things may not be tidied up, or automatically returned to the room from which they were taken. Cups and plates can wander from room to room, from shelf to table. There often does not even seem to be a person behind these migrations! Then things get lost, or turn up in very surprising locations and we find that we use a great deal of energy and time simply looking for things.

Generally, we reflect our surroundings in our ability to cope with life's vicissitudes, and in this context, chaos does not really assist our ability to be composed, concentrated or thoughtful. Those people who suffer from an over sensitized emotional life, may be much more prone to panic when the ordinary things of life are not kept in place. Orderly surroundings help to keep the emotions tidy. On the other hand, people who become avid collectors and find it hard to let go of anything also seem to be fulfilling a need of soul. They seem to have to hold on to rooms full of books, or cupboards filled with exquisite china because without these objects they feel insecure and exposed.

It can be a great help to homemakers to learn to notice the effects of order or disorder on the power of thinking. This can be used as a direct tool for helping children and adolescents cope with developing thoughts and feelings. One can actually touch the balance of soul by how one uses *creative mess* to stimulate or allows *tidiness and order* to offer stability and form.

For example, we do not usually allow things for which we have no use to clutter up the house. We discard them at car-boot sales, store them in the attic or give them away. But for children this may not be the same at all. They love their toys, often the dirty, broken, worn-out ones all the more for their familiarity. No parent would want to clear out a beloved, scruffy, ancient doll. Children are collectors by nature, reflecting many of their experiences in objects that they acquire on their path through daily life. But they also forget or lose things, which yesterday were the most precious things they owned. They have a huge flexibility and width of soul. It is therefore important to realize that too many playthings can hamper their innocent freedom, tying them down too early to the need for possessions. However, too few toys within a rigidly orderly lifestyle, may narrow their creativity.

Because of their spontaneous and imaginative approach to objects, children will always make a mess. Play can probably best be described as a *tidy mess* because everything is everywhere and just exactly where the child needs it to be. Such creative disorder is a child's paradise because it allows the imagination free reign. Objects can become whatever the child needs them to become. The role of the parent or homemaker is merely to ensure that this imaginative approach to the things of the home does not get out of hand. Not all rules can safely be broken and children have to learn this as they grow up. If this is not taught, the child's ability to respond to things appropriately may be affected and constructive play may become merely the making of a mess, destroying creative development. Now and again, order needs to be restored, allowing objects to assume their actual worldly value once more. Children who live in constant chaos may tend to have emotionally thoughtless reactions in situations with which they are unfamiliar.

Adolescents seem to enjoy chaos, sometimes apparently trying to create it around them and living in a deliberate mess. Then, with great gusto, one can find them blitzing the rooms, making them Spartan and bare. Given time, the mess will creep in and once again a massive clean-up will be instituted. The great swings of soul that rule the teenage years reflect in the immediate surroundings. Many young people express themselves very dramatically! Though it makes life unsettled and difficult for the homemaker, tolerance and even a level of enjoyment in the scene changes can be very helpful because this constant fluctuation demonstrates the developing soul body, or astrality. Human beings reach out to each other through movements of soul, and the young person needs to learn how to do this. The first attempts are often clumsy and show in irritating outer chaos. Gradually as the soul moods settle, so too will their effect on the home environment.

Though finding an object in their own chaotic bedroom may be very easy, in unfamiliar territory young people often cannot find an object for which they are searching, even though it may be staring them in the face! By offering assistance and encouraging involvement in keeping the home nice, security and balance will gradually emerge. We need to tread carefully in response to the tender soul of the adolescent but sometimes a direct request or giving definite responsibility may help to bring stability. Once again, observing the cause of the chaos in relation to the temperament and life experience of the teenager will reveal the real need behind the mess. It is usually better to tackle disorder tactfully than leave it to fester.

Where adults are concerned, the state of order or disorder in which they choose to live can usually be ascribed to upbringing. Having left the creative mess of childhood behind and survived the chaos of adolescence, one will settle into what seems the most comfortable state of affairs. This nevertheless reveals the quality and balance of soul. We make our nests to suit our temperament, inclinations and artistic leanings. However, we cannot really escape the fact that a mess affects our mood and comfort, whereas too much order obstructs creativity. It is best to find a balance between hygiene, which is a necessity, and absolute order that may inhibit freedom.

We can support the balance of soul by keeping order in the home. Unexpected things can be faced and dealt with if the physical means to do so can be found at a moment's notice. We assist creativity by allowing things to be used appropriately. Accidents can be handled and human weaknesses endured when one tries to act purposefully and think clearly. In this way, we can begin to transform ordinary experiences of daily life into soul qualities and so develop the skills to deal with the changing demands. How human beings transform life experience into qualities of soul can be understood by looking at how the microcosm and the macrocosm reflect each other. By understanding how alien substances, e.g. food and drink, are absorbed into the body and transformed into life-giving etheric forces, we can begin to see how life itself affects and shapes our innermost being.

The Question of Healthy Eating

The body instinctively *knows* how to respond to everything that enters the mouth. It is because of this accurate and instantaneous response that the right chemicals are secreted so that the living strength can be used in such a miraculous way. To find healthy and good food is becoming much more common than a few years ago. There was a time when most things on the shelves in shops or markets had some additive, preservative, colouring or flavouring. Fortunately we have become more aware of the ill effects of additives and so we can make informed choices in most food outlets. No doubt unadulterated foods are more expensive but what is remarkable is that one needs to eat less when the food is healthy.

Although we do not become what we eat, we know that we need to eat in order to stay alive. But do we realize that it is by virtue of the living nutritional elements in our food that we become more able to work and think? Eating gives us the possibility to remain alive but the *quality* of that life will vary according to what kind of food we eat. We can give ourselves more stamina with naturally grown foods and therefore a more wholesome life style than with foods grown with hydro-culture, or forced by artificial lighting, or those that have been genetically engineered. It is common practice, sometimes even legally required by law, to supplement foods with vitamins and minerals that have been artificially produced whereas they are naturally balanced and present in abundance in organically grown foods. Chemically fertilized foods contain a predominance of minerals as well as traces of the fertilizers themselves. These components cannot be digested and so the body tends to process for excretion only. In the end, very little life force remains to be absorbed. This is the reason why we need to eat many more slices of white bread than we do of brown. Moreover, if, when selecting the brown bread, we choose one that is made from organic flour, then we need to eat even less of it. It goes much further because of its etheric health-giving qualities.

Strangely enough, we often still hanker after fast-foods though all of them contain a variety of additives. We seem to have mislaid our instinct for the nutritious and are attracted to the colourful and exciting appearance of fashion foods. Substitutes flavoured to taste like meat can cheat our taste buds. But is it possible to cheat the chemicals that have to be secreted in order to break down these substances? Unfortunately this can happen, but only as far as the mouth is concerned. Saliva responds to the anticipation of the food. If we do not know what we are eating and imagine it to be something different, the beginning of the digestive process is not going to be quite correct unless our taste buds recognize the food and alter the chemicals that the glands have secreted. We can observe this when drinking coffee that turns out to be tea. Although we may love the taste of tea, by imagining that it is coffee we find it unpalatable. The saliva secreted is not the right one for the substance. On the occasions that this happens when eating food containing unidentifiable supplements or additives, it is dumped, incorrectly prepared, into the stomach to be sorted out by the confused digestive enzymes.

Another equally serious problem to consider is that pre-packed and artificially processed fast-foods often require very little chewing. This results in an over-worked digestive system, which, when it can no longer cope with the amount of unprepared substances, causes constipation or diarrhoea depending on the constitutional inclination.

Mineralized food materializes the life forces. Fast-foods, fizzy drinks and artificial nutrients give little or no etheric structure. The life force is either stuck in the material substance, or is absent altogether. Moreover, such foods are often irradiated for preservation, heated to kill all bacteria, and then cooked in the microwave. With so much disinformation given to the process designed for digestive purposes, is it any wonder that we are not as healthy as we might wish to be? The confusion of the body's responses can only lead to diminishing etheric forces and this in turn will weaken the immune system. What is more worrying still is that eating mineralized foods dulls our instincts for what is healthy.

The question we might ask ourselves is: What manipulates a whole civilization so successfully that we can believe that supplements are health-bringing, when healthy instinct tells us that natural food has all the nutrients human beings really need? Any additive to food has the world market behind it and behind that lies the subtle work of Ahriman. He has persuaded us that in order to ensure physical strength almost everything has to have its complement of vitamins and minerals. Even water is filled with chemicals, added in order to harden and protect teeth and bones. Certainly, in some parts of the earth, this may be necessary, but it may lead to a less flexible immune system. Artificial additives are rarely the answer to good health, because they so often bring side affects, which may manifest, for example, in obscure yet irritating allergies. Sometimes, merely by drinking pure water, these can very quickly be healed.

If we want to promote good health, then good food is the first step. The responses of the body will be natural and balanced and life forces can be released for its sustenance. Once we are feeling healthy and well, our whole life style will improve. We will be able to do things with more energy, we will consequently sleep better and so will be able to think more clearly. By eating healthily, the body can become a servant, rather than the master of life.

This is especially important when bringing up children or caring for old people. Ideally, little children should be free of the fetters that ill health brings. They need their life forces for learning about the world. Old people are sensitive. They ought to be allowed to live out the rest of their days in as much ease and comfort as their increasing frailty will allow. However, when we are in the prime of our lives, good food is just as essential. It is during these years that we accomplish our aims and ambitions. Because homemaking can be tiring and demands not only mental, but also physical stamina, we really need to work from a position of strength. Homes that can offer organic food as the staple diet are offering an ongoing quality of life.

The Question of Promoting Good Health

It is neither incorrect nor dramatic to describe the process of secreting body fluids as magical. Furthermore, it really is a miraculous health-giving process, our glands seeming to know how to deal with foreign bodies such as most viruses or bacteria just as efficiently as they know how to deal with food. We know that it is by producing appropriate antibodies that we can fight off disease. We feel the effect of their work because it sometimes makes us ill, and we know that this is a sign that the body is using life forces to deal with and to conquer the enemy. When this is successfully achieved, we find that our immune system has become strengthened, we feel very much better, and we no longer need to catch that illness for a while.

Because the world today suffers from so many forms of pollution, even eating the very healthiest of foods cannot always prevent illnesses. Ahriman may be trying to harden human beings into practising agriculture as an industry rather than caring for the earth as a living being, but Lucifer too, seems to be busy at undermining us. His lies are behind the belief that preventing anything that may make human beings suffer or experience discomfort is absolutely essential for a happy life. How aware are we of the deception behind our ability to ignore the fact that almost all modern medicine has been developed by inflicting pain on living creatures? The result of this moral confusion is that we take very poisonous medicines to cure us of both mild or life-threatening diseases, frequently without proper discrimination and generally with little information as to their side effects.

Fear of fatal disease is a very natural and healthy instinct, and when facing the probability of a serious epidemic the possibility for vaccination can be a blessing. Nevertheless, we should be aware that its specific job is to build artificially introduced antibodies that are foreign to the human body. This means that the vaccine succeeds by persistently irritating the immune system so that it has to work extra hard. The unfortunate result is that the etheric body becomes debilitated and when illness *does* occur we may have less power to deal with it. It is becoming more common to find diseases that are resistant to modern medicine. They have developed because of uninformed and too frequent use of antibiotics and vaccines.

Nevertheless, it would be true to say that medicine today is a marvel of human knowledge and perseverance. Because of the work of dedicated scientists, we are able to save many lives. However, recognizing that the etheric body plays as important a role in the quality of life as does the physical body, is essential. If the life forces become too weak, the soul consequently suffers a lack of vitality and we become unable to experience all-encompassing good health. If we need medicines, it would perhaps be preferable to take something that can invigorate the life forces.

Conventional medicine works on the premise that the symptoms must be eradicated. Then the patient is restored to good health. Complementary medicine, especially homoeopathy, aims to address the cause of the illness, and by stimulating the life forces returns health to the physical body. Homemakers of old often kept a store of simple herbal remedies that could be administered before an illness became serious. These herbs promoted health, as well as curing sickness. Homoeopathy can be a support to homemakers. Though visits to the doctor are necessary, they can be kept for serious illness and safe remedies made from herbs can be used as a supplement by the observant and responsible homemaker.

Treating illness with natural medicines may take a little longer, but the cure will usually be gentler and will always meet the etheric need. Deciding which medicaments to administer means that one has to use common sense. Some illnesses need one kind of treatment, others something entirely different. Common sense belongs to our instincts and works through our feelings, helping to meet needs wherever they arise with appropriate responses. Common sense can really work like magic. In former times people were instinctively able to understand the needs of soul each illness demonstrated and so were able to find the cure. We can infer from this that our instincts told us about the intimate and fragile connection between the material and the non-material within each human being. Common sense is an active expression of the spirit that lives in every human being. It is a practical demonstration of the power of transformation that lies as dormant potential in every human soul.

Transformative Forces

As we know, every human being is a spiritual entity incarnated into a physical body. How else could our hard bones and solid muscles get up and move about freely over the earth? When the spirit leaves the body temporarily, it lies down in sleep. As soon as the spirit leaves the body altogether, the body disintegrates. This is a prime example of physical substances transformed by living ether forces under the guidance of the individual spirit. A comparative example of transformative forces in daily life is that we are able to meet and respond to challenges and needs. We do not always know precisely how to act in the best way but we generally strive to respond positively. Whenever we achieve such a positive attitude, a transformation occurs because something close to love of the world around begins to flow.

A great expression of love is shown in the life of Christ, whose response to the world brought healing with his power to transform, which we understand as the miracles that he wrought for many. The blind were healed, the deaf given hearing and even the dead were raised. Wherever he went, he responded with love, miraculously appropriate to each destiny, showing how, with love, the spiritual inner self can overcome outer physical defects.

We can take this as deeply significant for the whole of humanity. Most of us are unable to transform the whole world, because we have chosen to be born and live where our destiny has placed us. But what we *are* free to do is to meet the needs wherever we are, and try to meet them appropriately and lovingly. Just as the body knows instinctively how to change the things that we eat, so too can human beings deal with daily life just as effectively. To do this, we can begin by approaching life with *loving observation*. The quality of soul developed from this attitude will eventually become conscious knowledge, which can be transformed into practical skills that homemakers can use as tools in everyday life. We often wonder how we are given answers to difficult situations without seeming to try to find them. It is also a fairly common experience to be taken aback by one's own wisdom and to wonder from whence the insight came. In former times, such instinctive feelings were revered or feared, for example, in the wise women or witches, who delivered insights in pictures and symbols.

We are no longer able to separate our spirit from our body as those ancient mystics could do. Moreover, it would be very difficult to live in a world in which science has become the foundation of thinking, if we were to deal with life only on an instinctual level. So in order to make progress, we can begin to use a *new intuitive power*. Though it seems to run contrary to science, it brings very effective results. For example, when one observes a little child who is always cheerful and happy, suddenly becoming withdrawn and hesitant about going to school, then one may respond

in an uncharacteristic way. Because one can find no particular reason for this changed behaviour, one may very well,
against all logic, simply let the child stay at home because it
feels right. Then, in the peace and security of the home, the
child can feel free enough to confess either to a guilty
conscience, or to being bullied, or to worry about something. One is consequently in a very good position to help
to put things straight. Another example may be that a
young person at examination time is obviously struggling to
deal with pressure. Though very clever and able, when it
comes to the crunch, he cannot seem to cope with the
work. Here too, against all logic, but from what feels right,
one may well react by underplaying the importance of the
results. Furthermore, by harnessing the support of the
teachers, one can offer assistance to the young person on the
threshold of life, who may consequently do well in the
examinations. Conversely, one may, when dealing with a
more robust character in similar circumstances, actually pile
on the pressure because this young person works best when
there are deadlines to be met. *Feeling* guides one in these
moments of decision.

As a final example, one may quietly observe the patterns
that occur in the lives of the adults with whom one lives,
and so perceive trends and inclinations occurring and
recurring. By pointing them out without judgement and
without offering any answers, new choices and opportunities can be taken. One can step off the treadmill and find
new direction. But *whether* one speaks out at all, *when* one
speaks, and *how* one speaks depends on *feeling for the right
moment*.

The new intuition is the ability to connect observations
by initially feeling and only then bringing thinking to bear
on what has been learned. Today our highly developed
scientific logic tends to relegate feelings into the background, assuming them to be woolly and unclear. Nowadays, too, instincts seem not to be working as effectively as

they once did. It seems as though humanity is slowly but surely being separated from the eternal guiding principles that used to flow into our souls from the spiritual world. Nevertheless, our ability to feel continues to be the transformative force that works between thinking and doing. We find balance when meeting the needs that life presents if all three share an equal role. Life at home can run very much more smoothly if feeling can flow between those who live together, so that responding to happenings can be the general tone, rather than reacting too late to disasters.

Feeling is a quality of soul. It is not the same as our emotions and moods. It is a state of awareness that has constancy and can be relied upon. Instinct, too, can be an extremely sensitive and useful ability because it offers instant answers, a gift that the body can offer to us. By learning to use these gifts consciously, the new intuition can become a sound basis for judgement in daily life.

The New Intuition

Odd and unexpected things that people do, feel and say can happen at any time. As has already been discussed, finding the best way to respond used to depend largely on what we called instinct. Today, however, when placed in unusual situations, we actually have three choices. The human soul encompasses three major forces with which we conduct ourselves in relation to the things that we meet. They are the soul forces of *thinking, feeling,* and *willing.* We can *think* about what has happened, *react* to it, which means using our power of will, or *experience* it by using our ability to feel. Generally we do all three but it depends upon our temperament and upbringing whether we lean more to one or to another. But what we do less and less, nowadays, is to react instinctively. We want to think clearly. We want our judgements to be as objective and fair as we can make them. Unfortunately, in the course of searching for objectivity, we seem to have arrived at the conclusion that feelings and instincts lack credibility. And so we have the tendency to go straight from thinking into action, and allow ourselves the luxury of feeling something about it often only after the event has taken place. It is as though feeling has been squeezed out, leaving the two soul forces of thinking and willing in full operation.

Feeling, however, is very important to homemakers. We know that it is frequently by allowing our feeling to speak to us that we can react appropriately. Feelings are able to mediate between the coolness of thinking and the heat of action because they are so versatile. Working through feeling is a valid method, provided thinking and willing can play their part in equal measure. We can begin to learn how to use *thinking with the heart*, another way to describe the new intuition, when we live through happenings by observing them with empathy. By allowing the effects to settle down in the soul and then letting them rise up as though one were reliving them in an after-image, insight and knowledge can appear. Finding the after-image means that one can actively relive an event, understand its cause and its consequences, and develop the insight to do this simultaneously. In the past, human beings could only do this with hindsight. Today, people may experience the after-image as a matter of course, especially those who work closely with other human beings. Homemakers are in the very fortunate position of working in the ideal practice ground of the home, where human needs and gifts can be expressed without inhibition.

One might imagine that dealing with life in this way would take up time and effort. In fact, this is not the case at all. Witnessing something with empathy means to accompany the event by observing correctly what is taking place, and this is the first step in making the new intuition of practical use. It asks for presence of mind, a quality that most homemakers have to acquire because needs change so rapidly in the passing of a day. The second step is letting it sink down into one's soul, which happens quite naturally. It is the third step that requires a small effort because one has to refrain from making the instant judgements that the intellect expects. One needs to *listen in* or *feel one's way*. This is the only part that does take some time. The after-image, which is the foundation of thinking with the heart, can arise only when the soul is open and undemanding.

Naturally, in moments of crisis, one has to act instantaneously, but this can become as insightful as a slower, more feeling-filled reaction when the new intuition begins to work. In the normal, more measured events of daily life, one can find the time to practise thinking with the heart. The understanding that comes with it is well worth the quiet endeavour.

We know how important it is not to over-react. Taking a breath before rushing into things always helps when searching for a balanced response. In the moment of drawing breath, the after-image can begin to work and intuition can be developed as an actual skill. Human instinct, as it used to be, can slowly but surely be replaced by a new human faculty of intuition. One of the consequences is that meeting needs becomes something done in freedom.

Finding Freedom to Meet the Needs

Freedom brings its price. In order to be free we must make choices, and the moment they are made, what we did not take up is discarded. This means making a sacrifice and every sacrifice always has consequences. Either we suffer the pain of deprivation and consequently lose our equanimity or we make the sacrifice in a mood of efficiency, sometimes even defiance. Here again, Ahriman and Lucifer twist the meaning of sacrifice into useless martyrdom.

Making choices, or sacrificing one thing for the sake of another is actually a free deed of love.

Thinking with the heart needs selfless and enthusiastic good will. Once we decide to work towards this new faculty then meeting demands can begin to have enjoyable, not only challenging moments. We can take a deliberate step towards intelligent choices based on observation and empathy and then wait to discover what the after-image can tell us. There is a seven-fold way of practising the development of such a free and lively approach to daily life. By taking it up in an objective way, freedom can become a new feeling of joy in the small things of daily life.

The first thing to aim for is good physical health. This means healthy eating so that less illness need occur. When illness does arise, using medicines that reinforce etheric activity is the wisest choice. Sleeping enough, taking exercise, finding rhythm in daily life, allowing things to happen peacefully are all part of this first step.

The second step is to recognize one's place as a member of the human race. Each individual is no better or worse than any other. This means that what happens anywhere in the world is as much part of one's life experience as are the things that happen at home. This attitude encourages compassion and empathy for all human beings and brings in its wake warmth of soul. Patience with people's oddities will also be one of its useful side effects!

The third step is to acknowledge the fact that whatever one thinks actually touches the object of one's thoughts as much as a physical blow, or caress. The fact that thoughts have power can be used as a force for the good. Sending positive thoughts into the world, to people who suffer, as well as to those one loves, and to those with whom one may find it difficult to live, can bring very satisfactory rewards. Sleep becomes wholesome and refreshing if one's thoughts have the wings of love to bear them. Moreover, many knotty problems in daily life can develop positive results when good thoughts are offered to their cause.

The fourth step is to acknowledge oneself as a valid and effective individual spirit. Holding fast to the conviction that the centre of consciousness is within one's own soul, provides a very firm anchor in the stormy sea of life. Self-confidence grows with the certainty of knowing the self. Knowing the self means to accept not only one's gifts, but also one's failures. To be human means to be imperfect and yet have the desire to reach for perfection. Loving the self makes it possible to love others because in their weaknesses we recognize a common bond.

The fifth step requires an adherence to resolutions made until a new resolution is taken, or a decisive alteration is made. To be able to hold fast to one's decisions, and yet have the greatness of soul to change direction if necessary, means that balance and flexibility can be practised creatively and without losing one's direction. This makes the fears and uncertainties of daily life recede because one will be creating one's own unique mission statement.

The sixth step is to experience gratitude for all living things, for life itself and for the world around us. Gratitude is an attitude of soul, rather than an action, and so paves the way for growth and change. It opens doors and overcomes barriers between people. Acknowledging each other's efforts makes daily life so very much more pleasant.

The seventh step is to recognize that these attitudes of soul enrich the spirit. By trying to live in this seven-fold way, the faculty of being in the right place at the right time will be just one of the tangible outcomes. The balance that all homemakers seek as being essential to their task can become as natural as breathing.

6.

Caring

Maintaining

Caring is a small word that contains a vast and complex number of intentions. Love, concern, attention, healing, devotion and respect are just a few of its aspects. Cleaning, repairing, maintaining, counselling, nursing, nurturing show some of its activities. Nowadays, people can become members of the caring professions whereas in olden days caring was understood to be vocational. It belonged to the feminine rather than the masculine traditions. Within the home, caring can be seen as an umbrella under which homemakers work, as well as a specific attitude with which homemakers approach definite tasks. To the homemaker, caring means to maintain the fabric of life, physically, socially and spiritually.

Maintaining the physical body is demonstrated by the renewal of the cells. Physiologically speaking, every cell has its own life span and will die at the end of its time, but this does not mean the end of the whole body. Different cells have different lengths of active life, but over all, the body renews itself completely every seven years, and though we never become someone else, we do not retain the same cellular structure all our lives. Our basic physical appearance does not alter into someone entirely different but we do change and grow, get fatter or thinner, and gradually age as the years pass. The fact that our physical body retains its basic form is because of the life process that maintains the form. If this process works too hard, then a tendency towards sclerosis, arthritis, or fixed codes of behaviour and a strong adherence to traditions prevails. If its activity is weakened, then disorders such as ME, Alzheimer's, and a tendency to poor memory can occur. Some cellular disorders, too, can be attributed to a poorly functioning process of maintaining.

However, not only the physical body renews itself all the time. The soul, too, continuously keeps up with changing and developing experiences, registering them and maintaining the new emotions and feelings that they bring. Maintaining the soul is the formative principle behind the human ability to keep a sense of self.

In human development, childhood is a time of growing, and the body is in a constant and obvious state of change. Parents and teachers are very important at this time because they offer a level of continuity governed by knowledge of life that can help the young child to maintain a steady and positive experience of self. In adolescence, as we very well know, the body's obvious as well as hidden changes can be dominating and uncomfortable. During this phase in life, an inclination to use too much strength to keep up with these changes can absorb the developing identity. Some people even experience this as a loss of self, feeling so taken up by the flow of life that maintaining their individuality may be threatened. They may consequently feel the need to hold on to outer structures or existing traditions in order to maintain a sense of self. Others are well able to hold on to their identity, so much so that egotism and wilfulness in daily life can become a god.

Within society, maintaining traditions and preserving old customs is not a new concept. Humanity builds its new forms on the strength of past experience. Within the home, this rule is equally valid. Maintaining a life style that respects old traditions but is not afraid of new developments can only be achieved by caring about life itself. Children who grow up in homes where life, people, and the environment are all afforded care and attention, can travel through the uncomfortable adolescent years with less selfishness and will arrive in adulthood with generous and caring natures. The social expression of the life process of maintaining is being true to the form without having to insist upon rules.

Order and Form

Maintaining sustains the outer form and shape of the body and yet it is an inner etheric process that is part of the immune system. In the previous chapter, eating healthy foods and using life-promoting medicines were discussed because they help the body to maintain itself, but they work from outside in. Maintaining ourselves means that the formative process within our ether body takes the life-giving substances and uses them to uphold what is visible and material in us, namely the physical body. The inner process of maintaining uses outside agencies and so it can very easily be influenced by the environment.

As an example, let us enter imaginatively into a state of illness, or emotional instability. What are the things that can give comfort, security and ease? They are the things with which we feel not only familiar but which lie in the area of traditions. We enjoy, in weak moments, the structure of rules and habits. Another example might be to imagine having to compose a rather difficult application, or to write an important letter. The very first thing one usually does is to find a million and one reasons to clean and tidy one's house, room, study, or garden. It is as though when trying to think clearly, we instinctively feel we need a clean and tidy environment. What we are doing at such moments is maintaining the outer shell of daily life in order to activate the inner thinker, or doer.

Daily chores have a very calming effect when one becomes overwrought, stressed, or angry. 'Work it off!' is an expression that says it all! Energy that needs an outlet can be very fruitfully used in scrubbing, digging, bread-baking, or other such challenging jobs. When confronted by unpleasant events that need to be dealt with in a constructive way, it can be very helpful to perform some menial household chore whilst deciding what action to take, rather than flying off in anger or retreating into defensive ignorance. The little mindless daily jobs are frequently the influences that prevent the web of the social life within the home from coming undone.

It is true that the material fabric of the home needs maintaining, but in an effort to keep the structure and the life style steady, so that thinking can be clear, cool and collected, one can enter into too rigid a pattern. It is quite possible to carry the art of tidiness and cleanliness too far! This is one of the hazards that homemakers face. In attempting to maintain an artistic, beautiful and shining home, keeping it clean can take too much precedence. One would hardly aim for putting the physical needs of the home before the human needs of people. A superb and hygienic home leaves one a little bit cold and can make one feel guilty about the all too natural mess that is made as we go about our daily lives.

The small chaos that being alive engenders is part of maintaining a living home. When one walks into a house that is uninhabited, be it ever so tidy, it does not really feel like home. As soon as one has moved a few things, fluffed up some cushions, spread out a few personal belongings and put food in the kitchen, then the house takes on the feeling of home. It is as though some living beings have been released into the atmosphere by carrying out these little homely acts.

This is, in fact, quite true. The living beings that make up air, warmth, earth and water have been freed from manufactured objects by the human touch. These beings are nature spirits who, in ancient times, were known as fairies, undines, sprites, pixies, elves, dwarfs and the fire-spirits called salamanders. Folklore is full of tales of hob goblins who lived in the hearth and kept the fire burning in a well cared for household, but extinguished it maliciously in a home where hate and resentment lived. Fairies were known to fly down from high altitudes to bring flowers to the garden, or blow away the precious seeds. Farmers used to leave out a little milk every night to feed the elves. Failure to do so could bring down a curse and then cows died and pigs were barren, and the fox ate the chickens! Today we talk of gremlins getting into machinery that simply will not work as it should, especially on days when we feel in a bad mood.

These elemental beings, in point of fact, do not possess morality. They are neither good nor bad, they simply are a part of the life body of the world, alive and active in nature, and are caged in the manufactured articles with which our homes are furnished. They live in the walls of stone, in the floors of wood, in the metal pots, in machinery, and in the water that flows from the taps. They live in the sand on the floor, which, when we find it outside we call earth, but when we see it inside we call dirt. Human beings have displaced nature to create homes and houses, castles and gardens, and in so doing have disturbed and often trapped the elemental beings. The way we handle the things we have made depends on our mood of soul, and the beings living in them will either help or hinder us.

Elemental beings reside in every artefact when it is made from natural fabrics. Plastic has none because it is so refined from the oil it once was, that any living spark has been removed. Therefore plastic can last for ever, unlike other perishable materials that we use to make things. One hears stories of people who love their old cars and like to think that they go on running because they are loved! This is not mere fancy. It works because the elemental beings locked in the machine work to serve the master who loves and cares for them. An affectionate kick can keep a washing-machine going for years! But that same kick, delivered in anger by a stranger will not achieve the required affect. However, even though we can keep things going with love, usually they also need practical care and repair.

The elemental beings crave recognition but cannot abide direct attention. By acknowledging their existence, we give them their rightful place in the order of living things. Homemakers are very familiar with the experience of flying through the chores when in a good mood and of being bogged down by them when resenting the work. It is as though invisible fingers lighten the load, or weigh it down according to how much care is given to the tasks in hand. Respect for these nature spirits allows them to work *for* us, rather than against us.

Too little care invites dirt and unhappiness. However, taking care to the point of preservation, traps life. If household objects are too precious to be used, then for example, children go elsewhere to play. They go to the homes where moving things around is permitted. A house where children cannot feel free enough to play is unlikely to be a very cheerful place!

Adolescents enjoy being different. They need to deny most of the established forms of their childhood in order to find their own relationship to what they consider to be values and standards. This is often demonstrated by deliberately destroying order within the home. Bedrooms become the centre of chaos, clothes strewn everywhere, washed when not dirty and worn into holes. All the rules seem to need to be broken. Whilst living in squalor, they demand to see the soul-cleanliness and spiritual order of the adults around them! The best way to tackle this is to respect the chaos in the private spaces but to ask for the maintaining of order in common areas. Calling upon mutual respect in the home can only be a good thing.

Adults who maintain an extremely structured home will often find themselves going out to other people's homes for their social needs. Maybe their own home demands too much because they have not really made friends with the elemental spirits living there with them. Older people, however, can often be very dependent upon an ordered and traditional environment. It is as though their loosened ether bodies have lodged in the tables, chairs and bric-a-brac that they so much cherish. Living with older people asks for understanding and tolerance of their real need to live in their own home for as long as possible, where their belongings are truly at home and where they can maintain them as well as possible.

Order and form need not be fixed down. Order actually means to return things to their place when not in use. Skilled craftsmen and artists work with this knowledge. To be creative one needs to know exactly where every tool, paint-brush or musical bow lies. So much energy, good humour and creative time can be wasted looking for a tool, a potato peeler, or a tube of paint. Keeping things tidy and maintaining them in good working order is a major factor in lightening the burden of household chores.

Maintaining the Home

Maintenance of house and garden is a concept well developed in homemakers. Cleaning, washing, ironing, as well as weeding, digging and lawn mowing are jobs that fill much of the week's work. The upkeep of the actual building, the household maintenance, replacing light-bulbs, and painting the woodwork, are just a few examples of maintaining the fabric of home. Some people find this delightfully challenging work. Others, having less skill to call on, may want to ask their partner for help. Children love being part of a maintenance session where hammers, nails and screws come out to make something old reappear as new!

The general household chores usually need to be done on a regular basis. Here is where *routine* becomes creative. In the chapter on rhythm it was discussed how experiencing the cycle of events helps to keep the balance between peace and action. But when it comes to cleaning, then the best way to tackle the work is by creating a routine. Routine need not be deadening and unimaginative. Anyone who has tried to keep a tidy, clean, warm and beautiful home as well as hold down a demanding job outside will know how exhausted one becomes if a certain routine is not maintained. As soon as regularity is upheld, energy returns. Work that needs to be done every day can become a burden if too much thought and too little practice are expended upon it. Routine means that the jobs can be done quite quickly and properly without too much thought having to go into them. One can be mentally creative whilst automatically running the vacuum cleaner over the carpet. One can plan one's shopping whilst the hands are busy at the washing-up. It is quite possible to help the children with their homework whilst ironing their clothes. But if chores such as have just been described pile up, then one has to give them the fullest of attention and then they begin to press on one's conscience, which usually leads to a bad mood!

Routine is a boon to homemakers. Doing a little bit of so-called unpleasant work each day makes the going so much lighter because we can discover that routine jobs are not as soul destroying as we have led ourselves to believe. They are, in fact, like the earth under our feet. We rarely notice it, and even sometimes dislike its dull brown colour, but without it we would float away or sink. Our entire security would disappear. Just as we take the ground for granted, so too can we take routine as our faithful servant and appreciate it for its true value. In this way, chores can be fitted *into* time, rather than *added* to an already very busy schedule.

In former times, mending clothes and repairing toys were as much a part of the work done at home as was the housekeeping. Today, trendy toys as well as clothes have driven out the simple life style. Our disposable culture has made repairing or mending an old-fashioned concept. We buy goods with built in obsolescence that last only a short time, and so we have to buy something new and up to date. However, our conscience pricks us at the vast natural resources that are being used up, and so we recycle things—tins, glass, paper, etc. Lucifer is having a little game with us! He encourages us to over produce, making us want more and more, and yet we could have long-lasting, beautifully made articles that we would only need to buy once.

In contrast to the modern desire for change, we value the antique so highly that we can collect perfectly useless things of beauty and maintain them lovingly within our homes, though we dare not use them because they are irreparable should they break. Our present culture is racked between over emphasis on heritage, which is Ahriman's contribution to the confusion, and our longing for the new and exciting.

These are conflicting trends that only a society as affluent as ours can afford. Poverty-stricken countries work according to necessity. One cannot have what one cannot afford. In poorer homes, things are cherished, repaired and used over and over again. Three children share one bicycle, a pair of roller boots is passed down from brother to sister. A new dress is new each time it is handed down to a smaller sibling who has never yet worn it. Desire for things becomes appreciation, which raises their value into beauty *and* usefulness.

Within the home, a new awareness of standards can be founded. Taking care to repair things because they are quality goods and *looking after* them, can become an example to children because they are in that marvellous position of being able to grow up to change the world. As long as the home perpetuates the myth that new is best, or that old is too precious to use, we make it very hard to free ourselves from the misdirection of Lucifer and Ahriman.

Repairing is a form of respect for nature spirits and for

humanity's ingenuity, inventiveness and artistic skills. We are all too aware that science has given us the power to destroy the world. As a balance to this terrifying fact, maintaining a home that teaches living standards based on respect for artefacts and the skills to mend and make, can only be a valuable contribution to life. Moreover, caring can become a natural daily attitude.

Caring for Each Other

Caring for each other carries a wealth of intentions. Obviously, when someone is sick, or in pain, or in trouble, we naturally extend our sympathy and want to help them. But caring cannot come to a halt when all is well. This would potentially lead to people only taking care of each other in a crisis, and yet we turn to others also when happy, or when something exciting occurs. Caring implies a continuous mood of soul but the intensity varies according to need.

Everyone needs someone to talk to. Everyone looks for a friend to share precious moments with. Everyone hopes to include someone else in a joke. Children have no difficulty in expressing this social need. They find a best friend with whom they share delightful secrets and painful woes. Adolescents can sometimes appear morose and solitary, hiding their need for companions who care about them. Loneliness can be a source of great pain in these delicate years. Because of their vulnerability, they often find solace in forming groups. This is the background to the street gang but also the more positive enjoyment of clubs, and team sports.

Adults like to think that they have reached the independent years but in truth, they have finally reached the *interdependent* phase in life. Now caring can come into its own. Mutual respect includes mutual care and concern. Without it society would falter and disintegrate, and without care and concern the home could not function as a social organism.

Homemakers know how careful one has to be in order to maintain a constructive and caring home. Caring need not mean fussing over someone, unless they clearly need it. It can mean to leave someone alone, to be available, to offer support, to ask questions, to listen, but most of all to converse. The art of conversation lies in opening oneself to the other's concerns and participating in them without taking them on as one's own. Talking to each other is the cornerstone of caring. By talking, we learn about each other, but we do not necessarily become dependent on each other. Conversing leads to *interdependence*, as opposed to *independence*, because we get to know each other inside out without having to live in each other's pockets! Interdependence is another step on the road to discovering the real meaning of love.

Dependence, Independence and Interdependence in Human Development

The manner in which human beings experience dependence has not always been as it is today. In far off times, people could not survive without the tribe. It upheld their security, judgement and physical comfort. The tribe, or extended family, nurtured and cared for all its members, representing the home and setting up a hierarchical system of government based on age and wisdom. From the tribe sprang the kingdom, the empire, then nations and finally, in our time, unions of states. Today, the dependency of large numbers of peoples no longer rests with justice, security and food. It rests on money. We have moved from the bartering of objects as a mode of dependence into one of tokens based on abstract holdings and market forces.

Individuals, too, have changed their experience of dependence. The shift from tribe to family gave a relatively slight change of emphasis, but within the last few decades, the family too, has grown smaller and eventually almost ceased to exist as the main centre on which to depend. Marriages are no longer for life, and rearing one's children is a shared venture between parents, teachers and child-minders, thus taking it away from the home as its centre. It is possible that because family forms and ties have become so transparent, the need for independence has become so strong. But it might also be that because the need for independence has grown so strong, the family has lost its powerful influence on individuals.

Human consciousness has undoubtedly altered since we made our homes in caves, or mud huts. Western affluence has spread its remarkable influence over the whole world, bringing in its wake a desire for material wealth and the right to ownership, and so destroying the delicately balanced structures that tribal or family forms had created. Nowadays it appears to be everyone for himself, and a drive for freedom of the individual to choose his or her own life style. Highly prized though it be, once independence is achieved it can leave one feeling cut off and lacking in communication with others. Independence is a two-edged sword that wins us freedom, but if handled for gain, rather than love, can lead to extreme loneliness.

Tribal consciousness gave us a feeling for the whole, a common source of standards and judgements. This could be called soul feeling or the *sentient soul* state of consciousness. One thought as a part of a group, leaving individual inspiration to the chiefs or leaders. Small children still function in this way. They leave all the decisions to their elders, feeling secure in their wisdom, unquestioning as to their parent's absolute authority. If a small child argues, it is rather to have this authority enhanced, than to quibble with it, an intention we adults often ascribe to the innocent infant, investing it with powers of reasoning that it has not yet reached.

From the tribal, sentient soul state of being, humanity moved on to the establishment of larger groups, i.e. states and kingdoms. Immediately, justice and decision also moved from the chief, or elder, into groups of councillors, or senates. Theoretically, anyone could aspire to a role within the nation if they worked at their grasp of politics and national interaction. This showed a development in humanity towards individualized thinking, and the intellect came into being, so one could call this state the *intellectual soul*. Adolescence mirrors this state of consciousness, because one is not yet able to stand alone, and yet determined to exercise one's own fledgling judgement against adult authority. One wants to go it alone.

Today we are individuals with a voice and a conscience. Though we still govern ourselves in states and with senates, many individuals are free to follow their own beliefs and convictions. In many countries the family no longer exerts pressure to conform to its standards. By and large, each of us chooses our own destiny. We have reached the stage of responsible awareness of the self in relation to the needs of the whole. This state of thinking can be called the *consciousness soul*. We no longer look to anyone but ourselves for what we encounter, and for how we deal with life.

Is it any wonder that the home has been called into question? Because the home has always been based on the family, must it become obsolete with this new leap in human thinking? Is it possible that the home is still a great need, and that society stands and falls on the way we have been brought up? A change in consciousness always means a change in outer expression of spiritual truths, but does it necessarily have to mean dissolving the stability of the centre in favour of the loneliness of diversity?

We can take as an example the individual development of the human being in connection with spiritual influences. As we grow from infancy to adulthood, our guardian angel alters his involvement from direct protection of the small child to a more remote influence that has to be sought by the individual. As an adult, it is necessary to ask the guardian angel for help, rather than merely expect it to arrive! In comparison, just as we know and trust our guardian angels, so too can we experience and trust the higher archangels to watch over the diversity of groups of souls on earth. Their task is to lead, guide and influence the healthy development of groups as large as nations because their vision is so great.

However, there is one high being, who, in this age of light, we experience as the power of enlightened thinking. He watches over individualization and independence of spirit and his name is the Archangel Michael. He is the great expender of justice, the angel with the sword of the light of spiritual thinking, who fights the dragon of darkness and ignorance. He holds the balance of the world in his hands, and is sometimes called the face of God. It is Michael who challenged Lucifer's enormous pride and threw him down from the heights of heaven unto the earth. His strength came from adherence to the creative centre of the universe.

In all mythologies and religions, a being of light who serves the spiritual freedom of humanity can be found. He may be called Apollo, the sun-god, who saw to it that the orb of life moved in its rightful path over the skies of the world. Or St George, who killed the dragon that ate up the life of the nation by devouring its virgins so that there could be no new birth. Or Perseus, the slayer of the Medusa, a ravishingly beautiful immortal, whose hair writhed in the form of snakes and who petrified the unwary person who dared to gaze on her countenance. Many were turned into stone until Perseus, seeing her reflected in the mirror of his shield, was able to cut off her head. However he may be portrayed, he is always the same bringer of freedom and light into the destiny of peoples and nations. Today, the light is very bright. We are learning to trust the human abilities of imagination, intuition and inspiration and because of this we reach into all manner of beliefs, some very safe, others very new and even doubtful. But we have the courage of knowing that an honest search will lead to the revelation of the spirit behind matter. This courage we gain from Michael who watches, particularly in our present time, over human evolution by offering strength of spiritual knowledge to individuals who want to assist this development. With his help we can understand that every change in consciousness challenges the old order. We cannot make progress without a certain amount of conflict and confrontation, but as long as this is treated as a positive dynamic that can add to our limited vision, rather than a reason to fight, we will continue to move forward. This holds good even in so small a society as the home. Serving Michael's call to the uniqueness of the human spirit is hard to fulfil and needs some help so that alienation need not be the sad outcome resulting from listening to Lucifer's pride, or Ahriman's doubts.

Independence that devotes itself to its own satisfaction shows that we have paid too much attention to Lucifer's whispers telling us that freedom means to need no one, unless it is to use those around one for one's own pleasures and gains. Avoiding independence and allowing oneself to remain embedded in the lives of one's blood relatives only, means that we have been led away from Michael's message of human development and buried ourselves in the group. Caring for each other's inner space and freedom of thought means that the separation that *independence* brings has taken a step forward into the mutual respect of *interdependence*. Having evolved into the state of the consciousness soul, we cannot remain embedded in the family or in the nationality in which we are born. We have reached the stage of sharing our lives because we *want* to do so, not because we are forced to do so.

Stepping forward from obliged affection into the freedom of caring and love can be painful and difficult. The social life at home often suffers under the pressure of people struggling to find their freedom within the totality of the group without upsetting the whole, or losing their individuality. Wanting to be a homemaker asks for commitment towards developing interdependence and sometimes this may mean turning to others for help on the way. Maintaining harmony when trying to uphold the search for freedom is a very challenging aim. With the help of the image of Michael and his brightness of thinking, we can find an inner source of strength against the threat of alienation and polarization within the home.

Counselling and Conversation

Alienation used in the context of the human soul is a modern concept. To be an alien means to be a stranger in a strange land. The experience of feeling a stranger to oneself is becoming a feature of the times but how can one be a stranger in one's own soul? Not knowing what to do with one's life, not feeling at home in one's country, or town, leaving one's friends for a new challenge because one can no longer follow the old, these are not unusual conditions to find in the modern human being. And if one searches for the reasons for these migrations they stem from the need to find one's true *soul home*.

This condition of alienation can become pathological and we call these times in life a period of mental breakdown, where maintaining one's sanity is threatened. The pain in the soul can be acute and the suffering is very severe. But less painful, though no less serious, are the times of doubt and uncertainty that plague ordinary life. Maintaining a home in which someone is going through such a difficult time requires a special effort from the homemaker. And should the sufferer be the homemaker in person, keeping the soul of the house together can be very hard. At such times the thing one can do the least, but needs to do the most, is to reach out to people who understand one's distress. The feeling of alienation can be so strong that it actually interferes in the ability to communicate. Talking ceases, one becomes morose, or trivial. Real contact fades away. The role of homemaker is a delicate one and needs to be maintained in order not to succumb to these stressful times.

There are a variety of ways to tackle psychological problems nowadays, and it is almost fashionable to have a psychiatrist or to be undergoing psychotherapy. There are times when it may indeed be necessary to go through regression therapy, reincarnation therapy, group therapy, and many others. We are conscious of the need to overcome alienation and so we entrust our most tender secrets and dreams to strangers because they are professional listeners. There is no doubt that in acute situations of breakdown we need the help of professionals. However, under normal circumstances, such assistance need not be our first port of call. What has happened to friendship? Is it always the best thing to ask a professional to lift us out of depression caused by deep doubts in our own validity and our statement of selfhood in the world? Why is it that homemakers, whose job it is to build bridges between individuals, can need to have recourse to outside agencies for guidance?

Precisely because homemakers are in the forefront of developing a vital new human faculty, their vulnerability will be all the greater. Approaching life today with an understanding that the state of the consciousness soul is still very new, and that we are in the process of *learning* to relate to each other with empathy but have not yet achieved this important step, can help to explain the longing for professional guidance. Acquiring the art of listening and speaking so that these can bring healing to lonely souls is part of the social art of homemaking, but when the homemaker is in need, counselling from outside the home can often open up a new state of objectivity. Stepping beyond the known boundaries into a free space, which is what counselling can offer, is a metaphorical image of what the soul is learning to achieve. We seek this condition in practice for becoming consciously in control of our own destiny, not in order to reach for the stars but in order to make sense out of the daily burdens that ordinary life offers.

Counselling may have temporarily taken the place of conversation as the healer. Nevertheless, this does not preclude the healing power of conversation, *real listening and speaking*, from being the most essential aspect of maintaining a sane and wholesome home. Trying to build a bridge of empathy between souls who feel, act and think, each in their very own individual free way, can only be of help in the effort to build a sane society. Individuals living side by side who experience each other as enemies to free self-expression can only bring destruction to the society that human evolution aspires to create. Everyone is different, individual and unique. Should we not rejoice in this wonderful gift of freedom? After all, what the eye can do, the ear cannot achieve. But is the human being whole who has only eyes, and no ears? Because a foot is not a hand, does this make the foot less useful? Different parts of the body are alien to each other but they are, each one, of primary importance to the healthy state of the whole.

We need each other to maintain our humanity. Without an appreciation of each other's differences, pains, aspirations and hurts, as well as achievements, creativity and loving gestures we lose compassion and take a backward step away from interdependence. The small steps that we take in the small society of the home can help humanity on the road from painful alienation towards a greater freedom of soul.

Sharing, Caring, and Responsibility

It is indisputable that having no home lies at the root of most social ills. Loneliness, carelessness, physical vulnerability and moral problems are difficulties that homelessness exacerbates. Trust, confidence, love and self-esteem are qualities everyone seeks, and they can really only be learned in a place of warm security and human interaction. Whatever an individual learns throughout life will have been conveyed to him through other human beings, or states of consciousness that other human beings have created. If, at the early stages in life, these lessons are taught with care and love, then the moral development towards freedom can be better achieved. However, it requires continuity, care and attention, and the willingness to accept that homemaking covers many areas of responsibility. By allowing these to become shared fields of activity, life skills essential for the creating of a healthy society can be learned in an easy and enjoyable way by children who will become responsible adults in their turn. To help this to happen successfully, someone has to be willing to be in the centre and carry the many needs of the small community of souls within the home.

Economic necessities that call the homemaker out of the home may be real and demanding. Sometimes, sharing this need with one's partner is not enough, or one may have no one with whom to share it. This fact of modern life does not help the maintaining of the home, but it need not be as big an obstacle as we have allowed it to become. Though the soul of the home asks to be filled by one person, the tasks that belong to homemaking can be fulfilled by more than one person. Job-sharing can be a reality within the home and perhaps become a role-model for a new society! However, this can only happen if the role of caretaker is taken seriously.

To begin at the beginning is often the best way to do difficult things. Caretaking begins with the very small child who plays happily, using household articles, boxes, dolls and model cars and at the end of the day retires blissfully to bed. Either the toys are left abandoned till the next day, or someone tidies them away, or better still, the parent together with the children makes putting them into their places an enjoyable part of bed-time. One need not be surprised to find that most young children will love this game. Touching, loving and lingering over beloved toys makes bed-time recede just a little, but it also becomes a routine event in the day. Little children, unlike adults, *like* routine. They appreciate repetition and find deep satisfaction in traditions. From a relaxed approach to keeping things tidy and making beds, small chores like dusting and sweeping can follow as the children get older. Making the sandwiches for school dinners, doing the dishes and eventually helping to prepare meals will no longer seem daunting tasks to the growing adolescent. These little household responsibilities mean that later on greater responsibilities can be handed over into practised and willing hands. Knowing that not only the house itself, the gardens and the cleaning need to be maintained, but that all who share the home also need to take care of it, makes everyone become aware that they are in the same boat! In this way, housekeeping can encourage mutual appreciation.

Commitment to the task of homemaking will help to answer the question: 'Who is responsible for the home?' Responsibility means to be able to answer for what happens. It asks for involvement and is one way of expressing interdependence. To be responsible for people or things does not mean ownership, but rather stewardship. The steward of old, though he did not possess the property, cared for it as though it were his own. Under the influence of Lucifer, we have been taught to despise so humble a role, and Ahriman has helped us to expect to be the owner of what we have and what we do in life. But in truth, caring for each other and caring for the home is the exact opposite of ownership and possession. We take care because we love and respect what we do in life. Being a homemaker can be compared to being a steward. To practise so selfless and exacting a task asks for consciousness. We cannot maintain responsibility unless we *know* those with whom we live. But really to know each other when everyone is trying to become a free individual, and so is undergoing varying states of mind and heart, can be a huge challenge. Fortunately, we can ask for help from our spiritual friends.

We can begin by, metaphorically speaking, taking the members of the house-community with us into our sleep. This means that before going to sleep, we consciously summon up an image of each member in our mind's eye. It is not necessary to spend a great deal of time and energy on this, if the pictures that are called up are vivid and alive. Then the souls of our friends or relatives will accompany us during sleep and allow the guardian angels to interact with each other. A feeling of connection, of being in tune with each other without obligation, will be the result during the days that follow. Being responsible can thus become second nature, losing its sting of anxious over-consciousness.

One of the very tangible effects of the joint working of the guardian angels is that one will acquire the ability to be at the right place at the right time. Before the days of the electronic baby alarm, mothers could utterly rely on this mode of communication and felt safely responsible for their children. We can develop this skill in a new way by conscientiously following the above practice. For those who work outside the home, acquiring this practical consciousness will help to avoid feeling out of touch with what is happening at home.

Maintaining a social home includes administration, an aspect of responsibility that can be shared and will give everyone a common picture of what it takes to keep up the physical fabric of life. Ignorance of financial matters is often the prime cause of irresponsibility. By encouraging insight into this field of homemaking a real togetherness can be built. Doing the administration requires a special consciousness because if it is not responsibly handled, it can cause disaster, but by sharing this task, not least by offering information, an appreciation of the individual need can come about and petty jealousy can be avoided.

Strangely enough, though money and administration appear so mundane, in practice, being open about them sheds light on deeply sensitive aspects of our being. How we use money, what each one has as needs, what little hobbies we enjoy, and what we think about each other, show up in expenditure and can be witnessed by the administrator. Because of its delicate nature, it needs great respect and tactfulness and then the power it can give us, which Lucifer would like to encourage, can be transformed into love and understanding. Interdependence is a reality when it comes to the money spent on housekeeping!

Responsibilities belonging to homemaking are manifold. When children are small, they need someone at home all the time. As they grow older, it is important to be at home when they return from school. This is the time of day when they need to off-load mistakes, or share their joys and achievements. School offers a wealth of information, experiences, social activities and life skills, and they fill up the little soul, which consequently needs to be unburdened, even of the positive things that have been absorbed. The number of children on the streets after school, carelessly wandering about in loud and sometimes destructive groups would be fewer if they had someone to go home to.

On reaching adolescence, a listening ear and a good sense of humour are still necessary, as has already been discussed, but now the addition of a certain amount of responsibility within the home becomes important. Learning how to manage on an allowance, learning how to judge the space and time needed for one's social life without neglecting one's working life are abilities that require practice. Learning these things at home from someone who can give advice, eases the path to adulthood. Encouraging the young person to take up employment in order to earn some extra money is all part of maintaining life. Young people who feel that their only expression of self is outside the home doing life-threatening or lawbreaking things, are young people who have not been offered responsibility for the real things of life, that is, for the livelihood of themselves and of others. Caring comes naturally to the adolescent who is encouraged to take responsibility for his own actions.

Recognizing the overall commitment and responsibility that belong to being a homemaker has the magical effect of lifting the curse of resentment and pride. The moment the task is accepted, ways to share it open up. A mutual acknowledgement of the validity and importance of every member at home will follow. Especially older people, like grandparents, value being able to contribute to the general household. Their tasks may need to be small, such as reading to children, or helping with homework, because their physical strength may not always be up to more strenuous jobs, but there can be a task for everyone at home, if all feel equally involved in maintaining this social setting together.

Interdependence is a practical expression of love. It offers a free space between people who want to interact. Taking care of each other, our homes and our aspirations maintains our essential humanity because it allows structures and forms to develop out of real tangible needs rather than imagined wants and wishes. Moreover, because the homemaker is also part of the house-community, one of the major problems of homemaking will cease to exist because one will know that one can ask for help. Everyone will be able to see and experience that maintaining the home in body and soul is everybody's responsibility. One will find oneself free enough to be able to offer help where it is needed and free enough to accept it when it is offered.

Caring is a much needed social ability. The future of humanity rests on this gift. Overcoming barriers of beliefs, customs, language and thinking can only come about if we care enough to make the effort. We can start with people who are near to us and so begin the slow change that society longs for.

7.

Self-Development

Growing

In the normal course of life, a human being goes through various states and conditions, each new experience adding to the mind's dimensions. Development is continuous. We never cease to grow and change as long as we are alive. Physical growth, however, does come to an end. We do most of our growing in early infancy and childhood, and in the average human life growing stops at the end of adolescence. We consider ourselves to have reached our mature stature by the time adulthood has come. In relation to the depths of the real self, however, we generally feel ourselves to have a personality that *is*, and that understands, as well as judges and reflects on the events that occur and that shape our lives on earth.

Seen in this way, growing as one of the processes of life clearly functions within the three dimensions, i.e. the body grows upwards, the soul and mind grow outwards, expanding with life experience, and the individual guiding ego grows downwards into incarnation. We talk about *growing up* in relation to child development. But we also know that the individuality *grows down* by the way in which self-control of the body is gradually acquired after birth. First the eyes, then the smile, then the neck muscles, then the arms and hands, then the back, and finally, only after approximately twelve months does the infant achieve an upright position. A *widening* life experience can also be readily grasped by becoming aware of the connection between learning and growing. These three-dimensional activities of growing come together in the human gifts of *walking, speaking, and thinking*. We share movement over the earth with the animal world, but uprightness, which is actually against the laws of gravity, intelligible language, which is conscious use of sound, and coherent thinking that controls desires, drives and instincts, are purely human developments. They demonstrate the fact that we are spiritual as well as physical entities.

The most active time of growing takes place in the first twenty-one years of life. These are also the years when the home plays a very important part in development. Healthy growth is dependent upon a healthy life. Harmonious development of soul is dependent upon a harmonious home background that corresponds well to a stimulating and broad-minded education. Healthy incarnation is dependent upon a sound physical body so that the spirit can fill the material house in which it has chosen to live. Homemakers can do so very much to bring about the optimum environment and in so doing are in the unique position of learning about human evolution in miniature.

We all have a natural longing to grow up, to become the self we know we really are, and we all have difficulties to overcome, and temptations to resist on the long road to individuality and freedom of identity. But for some people, incarnation and learning are much more complex than for others. For people with learning difficulties, caused by whatever circumstances, be they illness, birth trauma, brain-damage, genetic or otherwise, development is usually slow and needs a great deal of in-put by parents, teachers and sometimes even doctors. The growing self meets up with physical hindrances to incarnation and so needs help in overcoming them. Those who have disabilities have a far harder struggle to grow and change. Therefore, whatever is done at home, whatever opportunities can be given in the way of life experience, are vital chances to develop.

It is through development of the soul that the spirit

and body can be harmonized and life can become meaningful. The human soul is an inquiring, seeking, questioning, intelligent, open and eager part of the human being. We can awaken in the morning with aching desire for knowledge and wisdom, and find that at the end of the day we have achieved none of them. We can also awaken in apathy, wanting nothing and giving up all hope of any advancement. Fortunately, we usually wake up in balance with the self, knowing that the day will offer opportunities for growth and change, and though we may never reach our heart's desire, we may take small steps towards it.

Wanting to learn, hoping for change and growing in wisdom is a human spiritual activity This desire brought about schools, colleges and universities. It also created apprenticeships, training and practical learning. Furthermore, it is this purpose that makes ordinary daily life a great school of learning. Life experience is in some ways the greatest and most reliable source of growth towards self-knowledge.

Being a homemaker means that the latter source of learning is readily available. Where else in the world can so much variety and reality be seen and understood in so small and compact an arena? Life at home is *real* and what can be learnt from making a home is not only real but lasting in its practical wisdom. Everything is a source of learning, everyone brings a new outlook from which to learn, every day offers new insights and new experiences. No day is ever the same. What can be learned from the observation of simple everyday human beings, child development, illnesses and human suffering as well as new achievements and inventions, plus the unfolding intricacies of human relationships, can be found within the small setting of the home. Home is the world on one's doorstep, it is the university of life.

Preparing Children for Life

The desire for self-development is a healthy one. We are born with it as the inner purpose that helps us to achieve the milestones of early learning. It broadens into a wish to know, to discover and to become effective in the world at large. Most people continue to want to learn for the rest of their lives, some in academic study, others in a variety of directions and what one eventually takes up as a profession does not preclude the continuing of adult education. However, what one has been offered by way of education in *childhood* affects one's interests and confidence where learning is concerned.

It is important to realize that the very first teacher in life is usually a parent, and the most influential is the homemaker, the one who chooses to be at home all the time. So much of our values that we live by and seek in others are given to us in very early infancy. To be a homemaker means to hold the future in the hollow of one's hand, *literally*. What we teach at home remains throughout life. This is a challenge but also an exciting opportunity. How wide is our knowledge, how deep our understanding of the material and the eternal? We can only seek to grasp the important issues of life, knowing that we will never really understand everything. But we can exercise our minds as well as our hands and try to uphold the value of seeking the truth and appreciating the variety of ways in which it shows itself. There are as many ways to self-knowledge as there are individuals.

Because of the ideals that are born in us as faint memories of purpose from pre-birth, education today does not always completely fill the gaps between material life and the world of ideas. Young people whose imagination is vivid and who experience life with sensitivity may find that the gaps are too numerous or too vast. What they have learned in their years of formal education may not help them to manage the secrets of life. They may find that it is far more complex than they have been led to understand by conventional educational methods. The unfortunate outcome for these young people unconsciously dissatisfied with their education may be an escape into alcohol, or into other more damaging substances, such as drugs. The experiences gained, and which seduce into addiction, are not without spiritual reality, but the source is unhealthy and so knowledge gained by using these substances becomes a lie and usually leads to self-hatred. It can even eventually end in death.

Some young people explore this dangerous world in defiance, because they cannot find an edge of excitement any other way. But this is less common because this type of young person generally has high ideals and will be able to find a way out of the quicksand of illusion that Lucifer offers. Children who, early in adolescence, begin to walk this hopeless path, frequently blame their formal education for lack of stimulation, or boredom because of too little involvement from the adults at home.

There are, moreover, other negative influences at work in the world, and one of them is the modern need to be perfect in every way. This target can rarely be reached and so we seek and identify with groups that promise a way to achieve the greater good or the perfect society. The desire for this to happen is very human indeed. We all wish for a better world and hope that what we do in our life may help this to be realized. Many societies are formed to help the evolution of humanity and this can be very constructive. But under Lucifer's tutelage, some groups have grown up to encourage fanaticism, such as nationalism, or racism. The value of learning from different ideas is lost in sameness. Everyone thinks along the same lines. Definite knowledge of the self can be acquired in this way, but it will be entirely one-sided and will lead to a stunted power of thought and deed.

There are so many pitfalls into which our children can stumble in their desire for change and growth, that the way in which we bring them up, through stimulating learning and exploration at home, will become a sure and certain guide to healthy discrimination once childhood is passed and adolescence opens the door to new discoveries about life and the world. The example set by parents and other adult friends who are actively engaged in developing themselves can act as a safeguard when temptations rear their heads.

For this reason it is vital that within the daily life of the homemaker a space for learning is safeguarded. This may take the form of developing artistic skills, studying or taking up a craft. It may also be that contemplation or meditation fills that time. But whatever may be chosen as a source of learning will build within the home a lively and constructive element of discovery. Education can be found wherever questions are asked and honest answers sought. The outcome of self-development is enthusiasm for life itself.

As homemakers, we do not only try to foster warmth, beauty and the pursuit of truth, but we are also attempting to show that real goodness is a valid attribute to seek. To this end, if one has children, finding the type of schooling that can best continue the path of learning begun in the home is very important. But for everyone, be they child, adolescent or adult, to promote goodness in the world means to learn how to do things properly because one *understands how they work* and can apply that knowledge in daily life.

Bringing children into the world is a huge responsibility and educating them to do the good is part of the challenge. As they grow older, the step into formal education needs sensitive handling and choosing a school that can complement life at home is a serious matter. Good schools with broad-based curricula would be everybody's optimum choice. This philosophy is the basis of the Steiner Waldorf school system. The schools are pledged to offer an education based on harmonizing the arts, science and religion. The secondary, yet equally valuable quality that these schools encourage, is non-competitive learning. Each child is recognized as a unique individual who needs encouragement and enthusiasm from teachers and parents. Whilst the child is young, rather than feeding the growing intelligence with information, directing the ideals towards realization is tackled by making learning practical and applied, so that there will always be a complete comprehension of how things work. Subjects are taught in harmony with the child's growing powers of thought, and questions are encouraged as well as answered. Good parental involvement in the life of the school is also highly encouraged.

Once adolescence is reached and the intellect has fully awoken, information is increased, and sciences, the arts and comparative religions are studied in depth. At this point in child development a move to the usual state school may beckon. Some children want to specialize earlier than the Steiner Warldorf schools encourage. But for those who want to broaden their horizons with all that life can offer, be it art, science or an educated understanding of social, historical, political and religious development of the world, the Steiner Warldorf school is the best possible place to be. Young people are encouraged to think for themselves based on proper research. Moving into adult life from an education that is so comprehensive and stimulating can only be an advantage. Practical knowledge as well as the ability to think for oneself has been added to the example of open-mindedness within the home.

Moreover, those who are clearly intellectually inclined will feel encouraged to excel in whatever study they may choose, whereas those who may not be out and out academics will know that they have a valuable contribution to make in the world because they have been shown how to ask questions and how to find answers. The skills training they have been offered acts as the beginning of insight into their abilities and qualities. Most of all, they know that everyone is different and that it is by working with these differences that life has meaning and direction. Individual freedom of expression need no longer be swallowed up by drugs or alcohol. Where initiative and freedom of thought has been the foundation of life, as the years pass, seeking for increased knowledge becomes a way of life. Self-development begins to beckon and enthusiasm for learning can become a reliable friend.

The School of Life

There are many ways in which life teaches the lessons that need to be learned. One can go through life as if in a dream, letting events pass one by and feeling that one has little or no control over one's development. One can stop and stare at everything that occurs and so get stuck on something great and miss the little happenings that could have been significant. In such cases, one may feel that life is too directive and that one has no freedom within one's destiny. One can also try to take in as much as one can and allow events to settle in one's life of thought or experience and so find them useful as reference points when one reaches times of crisis. Making the effort to use daily life in the latter way means that one has entered the *school of life* deliberately.

There is as great a value in the lessons that one learns from the school of life as there is in academic study. Perhaps what one learns from being a homemaker would appear to be a jack of all trades and master of none, but the all round skills thus acquired in dealing with people, events, decisions and crises can hardly be bettered in any other situation in life. However, unless one consciously decides to learn from the everyday, one might find that homemaking is more than one can readily manage precisely because it is so varied and demanding. Then one may want to flee the home for an easier task in life, one where learning might be more formally offered and life in general more structured and less dependent upon one's own initiative.

Should the challenge be accepted, however, the rewards are manifold. The first and biggest of these is that one need never be bored again! Until one is old, there will always be something new to learn, to experience, to be amazed at and to enjoy. Needless to say, some of the lessons might be hard and there will certainly be a degree of suffering, but with an attitude of interest towards how human beings change and grow, darker times can also be learning experiences. Learning is not always pleasant and some of the most important things are learnt the hardest way.

Small children learn by osmosis. Later, when they go to school they learn from their teachers, who exert a natural authority by right of age and experience. Adolescents prefer to learn by bitter experience! They generally test their teachers to the limit, admiring most those who prove to have the greatest knowledge and expertise. As adults, however, we return to the small child's method, but this time in full awareness and with the humble attitude that everything in the world has something to teach us.

Businesses that run efficiently utilize this practical approach for training new employees and retraining the old. They organize workshops that aim to find practical ways of dealing with daily irritations or pressures of life. Latterly, they also use out-door pursuits centres. Here team sports, the physical challenges and the ordinary practical nature of the courses offered, address the common sense and general life skills of employees as well as employers. Because these activities take place away from the usual territory of the business, this creates a neutral and unbur-dened atmosphere in which the relationships of the participants can be seen in a new light. Interestingly, it is

often the management who seem to need and also enjoy
these activities the most. Weekend seminars are also on the
increase. The study aspect has to be done prior to attending
the actual courses. Assessments have to be written. Often
they are based on observation of the work that one is
engaged in every day. Learning from life is highly
encouraged.

At home, such challenges are everyday happenings.
Common sense is much in demand. And learning from life
can really hardly be avoided. The aspect of formal study,
however, can become a real challenge because one generally finds that there is so much of a practical nature to be
done that study takes a seat in the very back row!

The Question of Study in Daily Life

Although studying can often only be undertaken by making a definite programme that fits into the work at home,
nevertheless, reading is not beyond the bounds of possibility
and can be done in a less organized way. What a wealth of
learning can be had from reading books! When there are
small children at home, reading is not a luxury at all because
they love to listen to books read aloud. They are learning in
the nicest possible way. Nowadays, the width and excel-
lence of children's literature is phenomenal. Good children's books contain such a richness of knowledge and
wisdom that any open-minded adult can learn something
new from them.

As the children grow older and begin their own reading,
sharing in this educational process can be very rewarding.
Discussions arising from books that have been read can
open doors to sharing one's fundamental attitudes and aims.
Learning together with one's children is such a pleasure and
privilege. One may wonder if this is really learning. Did we
not go through all this as children? Of course we did, but as
adults we can distil a great deal more from observing how

our children learn as well as remembering everything that we have already learnt. Generations grow and change, one after the other, and learning with one's children or adolescents enhances what we may think we already know.

Focussed study is learning of a different kind. It has a specializing nature and can only be shared with people who are studying the same thing. It requires discipline and time, something that can only come into effect successfully once the children are older and can respect the need for such an activity. However, in homes where adults live together, study can become a social event. Sharing what one has learned enhances the knowledge gained and offers challenges to the other people with whom one lives. Discussion is fun, and why should learning, challenging as it is, be dull? The most lively elderly people are often those who have made the study of humanity a lifelong interest.

Learning also happens through cultural stimulation. We know that visits to theatres, museums and galleries provide us with spiritual nourishment, but making a point of exploring also those cultural events in which one may have had little interest offers learning opportunities that can be invaluable. The new and unknown can turn out to be inspirational as long as it is approached with a questioning attitude and the openness to discover hidden or perhaps obvious qualities. Here, taking the family along is fairly easy. The resulting discussions are moments of consolidating the intellectual or social lessons that have been learned.

Most homes encourage visitors and friends. Meeting new people, sharing one's thought, experiences, hopes and fears are all learning moments. No two people will have exactly the same reaction to events. Observing and listening to other people's life experience teaches so much, especially if they come from a very different cultural background. But even those people who may share one's own culture vary in their interpretation and feelings of life. Hearing a biography or seeing how a friend deals with pain, or sorrow, can be a very great lesson. These are all small steps on the road to self-development and self-knowledge, and if they are consciously cultivated and deliberate attention is given to every happening, wisdom will begin to shine in one's daily life.

To make life experience conscious so that it compares to actual study asks for a commitment. One can either deliberately share the little experiences and highlights of daily life with another person in order to objectify them, or decide to look back over one's behaviour during the day, step by step, judging neither right nor wrong but carefully observing one's activities, thoughts and feelings, before going to sleep. By doing this with decisive regularity, a practical self-knowledge can begin to grow. Gradually, one will learn to know oneself in a very new and encouraging way. However, complete honesty has to be cultivated in these reflections and withholding criticism is essential. Rather the desire to do better the next day is required.

Another focus may be to form study groups on subjects that are of particular relevance to one's daily life, i.e. child development, psychology, homemaking, philosophy etc. These create occasions for meeting up with like-minded souls who are walking a similar path of development and interests. The stimulation and knowledge gained from group work is enormous. Adult education classes or taking up correspondence courses can also focus one's areas of learning. These may take the form of learning a craft, or working towards gaining new skills in art or design. Not all formal learning is purely academic.

Whether it be through study, or daily life experience, homemakers have a distinct advantage over other people in that they can arrange their time to suit their responsibilities! This may mean that learning together with one's children is what suits the present time, or it may mean making formal arrangements with childminders or partners in order to study, but where there is an interest in learning, the time can be found. The small sacrifice of waiting until the moment is right for beginning to study does not take away the opportunity to learn from daily life. It will only add maturity to one's interests.

Development in History

The question still remains: Why should we bother? Why should anyone want to develop him or herself, to gain more self-knowledge or to change in any way? We have been through infancy, schooling, perhaps also university and now are adults living the life that is destined for us as best as we can. Society offers certain life styles, from which we can choose, and so we go from one set of circumstances to another, hoping that we can make as good a living as possible out of them.

And yet, as homemakers know only too well (and may suffer as a result of this feeling), it is not uncommon to find that such a humdrum approach leaves something vital out of its plan. There is a lack of stimulation for the inner self if one lives so plainly. Almost everyone would like to become something and this kind of ambition is extremely healthy. This is what has made humanity progress since the beginning of time. The story of Adam and Eve in the Garden of Eden tells how they longed to eat of the fruits that grew on the tree of knowledge. Taking this knowledge unprepared led to their downfall. But the aim remained and the myth actually lives on in everyone as the wish to better oneself as a human being.

We used to learn from gurus, great prophets and teachers. Before that, if the myths are to be believed, we learned from the gods themselves, who came down to earth to teach us how to till the soil, mend and make. In those days it was not scientists, who are people of earthly knowledge, but the gods themselves, who inspired the great inventions, the most fundamental of which, like the wheel or the plough, still cannot be improved upon. Today we admire and respect the specialist, and the smaller and more defined the area of study, the greater we admire the expertise. Because of this fine intellectual development, we expect everyone to go to school and to be able to read and write. Education for all is common, especially in the West, though in other, less advantaged countries, education may not yet have reached every person. With the current emphasis on learning, the intellect has grown. More and more people can have finer and finer specialized knowledge.

The intellectual approach to life, however, has the tendency to become very selective and to want to prove everything before being able to absorb it. But proving often closes a door. Growth and progress, however, are dependent upon the ability to question everything. Allowing there to be things in existence beyond our present ken, allows development and evolution. Science has taught us to think precisely, accurately and analytically. Nevertheless, in order to understand correctly, we have to take in the unexpected and the unaccountable as well. Then, by using the methods of thinking that science has given us, we can begin to discover the *invisible that we know also exists as definitely as does the visible*. This type of approach, which can also be called ordinary human curiosity, is what the great fathers of psychiatry employed in order to discover properties of the human soul, a very good example of something we know exists, and yet cannot prove in any material way.

There was a time at the beginning of the twentieth century when wanting to know about spiritual matters was considered ridiculous, or even quite mad. Only wealthy eccentrics could get away with diving into the invisible aspects of life. Nowadays, exploring the invisible is becoming less ridiculous and more acceptable as genuinely valid knowledge but it is still in its infancy as a science. Nevertheless, with its new found credibility, we are becoming increasingly aware that there is more to life than meets the physical eye.

That there is infinitely more to life than what we can touch, see and feel, is nothing new to the homemaker. Working in the home means that one is dealing with the invisible all the time. Though apparently working with very practical things, the homemaker is nurturing the growing and developing souls of all who share the home. If one is occupied with such essentials of life, needless to say, one arrives at the point of having to work at developing one's own soul. To do so means, first of all, to get to know the self. Self-knowledge, as the saying goes, is the beginning of wisdom. Because we want to grow, we can overcome any fear of being ridiculous when we start to explore the invisible influences that are around us in the world and so also in our homes.

There are many ways to tackle and explore the world of the invisible and to find a new relationship to the gods who once were our guides and leaders. But the first step is to *want* to know them. From that moment on, small things will begin to shine up in ordinary life and what seemed senseless will start to be filled with meaning. This does not mean that science loses its validity. But until we unite the two, we will only experience half of what there is to know. To become a good homemaker we hope to become a good psychologist, a wise counsellor and a practical person, but these attributes need to be learned, like everything else in life. Self-development means to strive for knowledge, wisdom and practical gifts. Self-knowledge means to accept one's failings and still go on trying to grow and change.

Finding Direction for Self-Development

To develop the self needs a direction. Dabbling in too many different theories and philosophies may create confusion and put one's identity at risk. Finding a reliable and spiritually honest way forward is not easy because there are many real and valid approaches to spiritual progress. Some people may choose the path of religion, finding a persuasion that answers their questions most effectively. Others may seek religion not so much to answer questions as to light up the existence of a world of the invisible.

Bringing religion into the home is a difficult subject nowadays. Because of the many ways in which religion is expressed, sometimes unfortunately in a rather inflexible way, it is quite common to reject them all as troublesome imaginations. The other extreme is to adopt one method as the only way in which to worship. Because we want to encourage freedom and an open mind, no homemaker who takes this seriously would want to introduce a dictatorship into the home. And yet, making a home that excludes the spiritual aspects is incomplete. Therefore, if one wishes to follow neither of these extreme options, how can one hope to bring a reverential attitude into one's daily life? Perhaps it would be more helpful to seek a spiritual reality that can be recognized as an expression of truth, rather than throwing the baby out with the bath water. Would it not be true to say that the many methods and dogmas that we call the various religions have more to do with human *interpretation* of these truths than with the truths themselves? The variety of religions that we meet is due to humanity's ability to understand things differently.

As soon as a belief becomes a dogma or takes on the sheen of fanaticism it falls down from its spiritual reality into Lucifer's stinging grasp. The spiritual companions that accompany us throughout life are there to help us overcome these tendencies that follow human beings in their search for self-development. The Archangel Michael in particular, with his task as the spirit of the Age of Light in which we live, can come to the aid of individuals as long as a healthy sense of curiosity and the desire to uncover what lies behind dogma and religious fervour are cultivated. Where an open mind and an honest approach to religion are at work in the home, the harder, more confining aspects of religious interpretation will be unable to take root. The natural human purpose, however, which is to love, uphold and respect one another, can find rich and nourishing soil in which to grow and bear fruit.

Religion means, to *re-link*, to find one's way back to the creator power, or god-head. Little children are naturally religious. They *know* that they come from God. As they grow, the world around them has the choice of reinforcing, reinvesting, ignoring, or ridiculing their innate belief in the world of the spirit. We are all a product of our upbringing when it comes to matters of religion. Therefore, the more freely and warmly we allow our children to meet the life of religious belief within the home, the more we uphold their freedom.

Another way to open the door to the spirit is to find a direction of thought that takes spiritual matters seriously. Once again, many doors are open. Some follow ancient spiritual guides from the East, or from Native American traditions, others take up spiritual teachers of old in a renewed form such as Rosicrucianism, or Theosophy, Feng Shui or Zen Buddhism. Some search for earthly advancement and so follow the traditions of Freemasonry, which has, in fact, a very ancient North African and highly spiritual origin. Others may seek very modern experiments in spiritual control such as Scientology, or Transcendental Meditation, both of which can give great worldly power. All are a search for the truth about creation and human spiritual development.

One of the most modern and tolerant, as well as morally

courageous ways to self-development is the path of Anthroposophy, or spiritual science, a way of learning that Rudolf Steiner imparted. By the depth of his understanding of evolution both spiritually and historically, all the streams of truth that have rung the changes throughout human development are brought into perspective of each other and can be clearly comprehended by any thinking person. Through spiritual science, natural science finds its complement. Understanding the material world that science has uncovered reaches further into reality when spiritual science comes into play so that the invisible can be made comprehensible too. Natural science, if pursued seriously and logically, can only answer the things of the earth. But we would never understand the human being if we only accepted the physical parts. Therefore, because we recognize that human beings are also spiritual entities, we can develop a rounded understanding of how to live. Spiritual science can be studied. It can also be applied, thus adding vitality and meaning to life. Studying spiritual science can open the door to understanding the real task of homemaking, as it can to every human developmental aspiration.

As soon as something starts to become spiritually strong, Ahriman and Lucifer begin to work their temptations and powers of destruction. They would not like to see humanity practising a living understanding of the spirit in matter. The risk that we would become like unto god, is too great. Ahriman sets out to make us believe that absence of a religious life is the only way to bring up children to become free in their choice of moral integrity, whereas the truth is that absence of moral example means that choice is made far more difficult. It is very difficult to make proper informed comparisons if one has nothing to compare. Lucifer, on the other hand, makes us explore so many spiritual paths that in the end we no longer know what we think and are in danger of throwing out all spiritual advancement, or adopting one persuasion that dictates the way to live.

Spiritual science seeks ways to keep to the middle path. By acknowledging the great debt we owe to natural science, and using the expertise we have learned to discipline our powers of observation and deduction, spiritual science sets out to teach us to observe on the basis of what *is* and then to think for ourselves. This is the greatest freedom, e.g. to know what to ask, how to observe and so to discover what one can truly believe and practise because it is based on one's own experience.

Learning in the Home

Home life is so varied that the opportunities for learning are present all the time. If one is so inclined and by using imagination and a sense of humour, one can learn from shopping, cleaning, cooking and balancing the budget! Experimenting to find new and better ways to manage the home can be quite interesting if approached with forethought and determination. However, one must never forget the people with whom one is living. Their needs, inclinations, potential and aims are the source of one's gathering knowledge and wisdom. By doing social things together, a path can be opened to new experiences and widened knowledge.

A very enjoyable way to learn more history and geography, as well as foreign cultural heritages, can be had by going to other countries for one's family holidays. Camping can teach one all there is to know about survival! Depending on one another's skills and knowledge of nature demonstrates how societies are made and destroyed. Group holidays with friends are tests as to one's real social commitment. Reading up on the places one intends to visit is a wonderful way of learning about the world. Usually, holidays are fun, and those that include disasters are often the most memorable! One feels one has learnt so much from them. Adapting holiday plans as the family grows older and interests change also provides learning situations. Sensitivity, as well as the spirit of adventure, are kept well and truly alive.

Holidays at home are times when the routine and rhythm are open to change. Different things are done, meal times fall as it suits, the house gets painted, the garden dug, new things planted; there can be time to experiment with cooking different dishes, and one might like to sleep in. With some imagination and adventurous daring, these too can be times for learning new things about the home and the house-community.

The key to learning at home is *curiosity*. As long as one is interested in people, and things, life can never be boring or static. Side by side with human interest one can place the science of *observation*. A keen and intelligent use of curiosity opens doors to new worlds of possibilities. The soul can expand into imagination. Contrary to popular thinking, directed by Lucifer's mischief, imagination is not silly and vain. Imagination is the result of a lively and colourful soul activity that arrives in our consciousness as new pictures and thoughts about people and things, about life in general. These pictures and thoughts are as true as the moral feelings that religion can give us. Homemakers with imagination can link souls. We can understand each other by having a little bit of imagination, and nothing can be humdrum and dull when this colourful aspect of the soul comes alive. Learning in the home from all the little, funny, ridiculous, tragic and weighty things of the every-day liberates the soul and is a constant and creative spur to the imagination.

Opening the Soul

Generally, we live our lives in contact with other people, sharing the home and working at jobs that bring us into relation with others. Usually we enjoy this human warmth.

But there can be times when other people come too close and constructive objectivity is swallowed in clinging emotion. Or we can lose ourselves in work, forgetting to keep up proper contact with our friends and allowing it to become the main aim in life. Homemakers may have days that seem to be ruled by one extreme or the other, perhaps because working at home can become somewhat too solitary in its responsibilities. At such times, curiosity for life seems to dry up and disappear, and this results in the soul closing down, building walls between the self and the world around.

The greatest human tragedy is when the soul turns in on itself. Imagination becomes dry, inspiration fails and intuition becomes self-seeking desire, or annihilating self-criticism. When this happens we recognize ourselves to be undergoing breakdown or deep depression. Coping with depression or low self-esteem by oneself, with no other support, can be very hard and sometimes this leads to the wish to escape from life's burdens. At such times anything that seems to lift the mood may appear to be a good idea. Alcohol, of course, does this very well! Homemakers, by the nature of their vocation, can come under enormous pressure, and do spend a lot of time alone at home. In our society alcoholism is fairly common and is the source of a great deal of unhappiness, especially for children. Needless to say, the damage to home life is untold. Fortunately, there are degrees to this condition and if one is awake to one's inner needs, desires and aims, one will be able to recognize when one is embarking on a slide into misery.

Usually, however, one avoids resorting to such measures of escape. But one can still be suffering from soul weariness. Closing down can show in a loss of curiosity, in doing things mechanically, in a wish to throw everything away for which one has worked so hard in the past, and to begin a new life away from it all. This is quite common, especially when the children have grown up and left the home and one has to find a new direction within the task of home-making.

When crisis arrives, to free oneself from preconceived patterns of living, to open up one's life of soul, to arouse one's healthy and natural curiosity, requires intervention, and so we seek for a suitable therapy to re-enliven the soul. There are many forms of therapy, but the best are those that stimulate not only the thinking aspects, but also the feeling and the willing parts of our soul life. These are the therapies that work through the arts, e.g. art-therapy, music-therapy, sculpture-therapy, movement-therapy, etc. They work on the imagination. They activate feeling by artistically stroking the soul until it can live in vivid and creative movement once more. The insights that one can gain about oneself by embarking on an artistic exploration are stag-gering and exciting! New life comes into being, new energy and a new perspective on one's knowledge of the world around one. Art activates observation. One has to practise *seeing and hearing* as if one had never seen or heard before. Through the arts the soul is reconnected with the body and the spirit.

Homemakers are artists. Keeping a warm and beautiful home, facilitating human growth and potential, caring for the house and garden, are artistic activities. Focussing this artistic advantage on one or the other recognized art form brings a release of tension and can help when a new lease of life is needed.

The physical therapies do something quite different. They bring one back into touch with oneself as an indi-vidual being. It may at first appear to be pampering the body, but in fact, through our sense of touch, we know where the world begins and the self ends. Depression, or stress, push one out of touch with this essential experience, causing so much emotional tension and mismanagement. By means of the tactile therapies, the tired homemaker, crabby and critical, can be revitalized into the warm, caring interested person by regular treatment of massage, acu-puncture, or hydrotherapy.

The benefits of therapy are, of course, not confined to homemakers alone. But if one has chosen to take up the task of homemaking in the society of today, with all its pressures, demands and critical attitudes, then it is not surprising that one sometimes needs something more than one's own spiritual striving, interest in learning and curi-osity about life.

Education sharpens the intellect, stimulates thinking and makes one feel alive as a spiritually seeking person. Therapy softens the bright light of thinking and the hardened con-tours of the soul so that feeling can live in the daily tasks, imbuing them with warmth and meaning. The world and the self relating to each other is the very positive outcome of these different spiritual activities.

The Necessity for Learning

If we listen to Ahriman and Lucifer, who speak so logically and persuasively through much of our everyday lives, then we may be led to think that learning about the inner aspects of things could be a waste of time. They are very busy telling us that there are two basic outlooks that one can adopt when approaching the development of the self. One is to explore the world of matter for one's own physical advancement, which we call materialism. The other is to acknowledge the invisible influences that also exist and find a way to learn about them in order to influence humanity as a whole. Should one decide to follow materialism, it is possible to arrive at a world for which there is no future and no hope. After all, matter must, by its temporal nature, die and disappear in the end. The other way leads us to a world controlled by an invisible dictatorship of wants and wishes. As long as one thinks that matter is all, then one need not care about the future, other than to preserve one's wealth, health and fitness. However, the task of homemaking is to nourish the eternal free spirit so that a new social impulse can grow.

The physical aspects of life do, of course, matter. We need our bodies to live. But what really gives us hope for growth is what we experience in our souls, and strive after with our spiritually unique individuality. We know, each one of us, that to be human is a privilege and that the world depends on our commitment, our involvement and care for its physical, social and spiritual well-being. No animal or plant or stone can advance the world one tiny bit, or destroy it, for that matter. But we human beings have the power and the control.

With such a huge and awe-inspiring responsibility how else can we hope to help humanity and the world on its way but by learning more and more about life, both physical and spiritual? Only with true and sincere knowledge can the indifference that materialism encourages be overcome. To care for human development is to take yet another step on the road to love. If we were not to care, eventually we would lose our curiosity and become dull, filled with apathy and boredom. Most homemakers, especially those who are parents, dread the moments when children announce that they are bored. Boredom leads to mischief because so often behind boredom lies dullness or lack of initiative. In the home where curiosity, questions and exploration are examples of the very life style, children will find it hard to be bored.

Setting out on a path of learning fills one with vitality. As soon as life is astonishingly interesting and hides its secrets only so that we can enjoy the search for their revelation, a new life fills the soul. The light of intelligence is lit and shines out into the home, brightening the lives of everyone. Living with someone who enjoys life, wants to learn, strives for knowledge and finds everything fascinating and worth knowing, is very pleasant indeed! Joy can spill out into the environment, filling the other members of the house-community. It banishes carelessness and superficiality and encourages growth and potential in everyone around. The joy of learning lies at the root of the development of civilizations, at the root of group dynamics, at the root of individual potential and at the root of a happy home.

Happiness opens the door to others and as soon as others enter one's life, change comes about. We cannot remain the same, untouched and unaffected by our fellow human beings. Interaction with other people leads to growth. An open mind towards humanity with all its vagaries and anomalies eventually leads the individual towards the achievement of self-knowledge and real wisdom.

The world of matter and the world of the spirit are complementary. The one does not exclude the other. As responsible human beings, learning about the world around us gives us mastery over it, not in order to exploit it, but in order to care for it and nurture its potential. All inventions were once spirit in the form of cosmic thoughts that individuals developed out of their understanding of the material earth and its wonders. As long as we remember that the spirit acted first and that the machine arrived through our human knowledge of earthly things, then we will always have complete freedom and need never be chained to materialism.

Asking apparently impossible questions inspired the great scientists as well as the great spiritual leaders. Today any one can ask impossible questions knowing that with the help of spiritual science these questions can find answers that are spiritually sound and practically applicable. Learning to observe the facts, so that a healthy discrimination between what belongs to the earth and what belongs to the spirit is activated, leads to understanding how they work together. And the nearest example of this is the human being in whom matter and spirit work together.

Homemakers are privileged human beings. Their work

lies in both worlds. Bringing up children means to assist human development, which is a spiritual activity. Taking care of the home and its environment means to work practically for the health of the earth and society. Living with other adults means to be open to human potential. Keeping an open mind is a fundamentally human attitude and is the foundation of self-development and real spiritual knowledge.

8.

The Social Art

Reproducing

Connecting art with ordinary life is a relatively new idea. Art used to be something one did if one was an artist, or if one wanted to be an artist. Art took one away from ordinary life into a vast arena of the new and untried, as well as unconventional experiences and unexplored vistas. To be *artistic* meant to be strange and exciting and also a little eccentric, vague or different. To be social has quite different connotations. We understand this word to encompass warmth, tolerance, understanding and acceptance. A *social* person is someone who likes other people, knows how to behave in company and is popular with everyone. Is it possible, therefore, to put these two outlooks on life together? Can anyone be a social artist?

The art of living, on the other hand, is not a new idea. The time of the Renaissance was devoted to the idea that art should fill every possible corner in life. But social equality or common standards of living were unheard of. Nowadays, we are fired with the ideal of a democratic society, of social organizations that take responsibility for the values and standards of life, but to practise an artistic expression of them is not seen to be necessary. What we *do* want is to live in a world where the freedom we seek is handled delicately and with sensitivity. To become a social artist implies dealing with practical situations so that everyone who is a part of that social space can become co-creative. It implies more than one artist at work, revitalizing the life style.

Where else does co-creativity bring about new life? In a more personalized way, when reproducing our own human kind. The spiritual creator-powers work in physical matter during the sexual act so that conception can take place. In times gone by, the two sexes were accepted as being necessary for the sake of perpetuity and were recognized as being a creative duo gifted by the gods. We used to cohabit in order to have children, to produce our species. In very far off times, children were conceived seasonally. We have travelled a great distance from this ancient tie with nature and spirit, and today we use our sexuality for pleasure, often preventing any resultant new life. We do not always appreciate, or even value the opposite sex, sometimes going so far as to deny our own sexuality. We are definitely no longer connected with the seasons since children are born at any time of the year. Furthermore, in many parts of the world, we can *decide* to have them. The culture of today and the scientific expertise that humanity now controls, allow us to arrange for conception and birth as well as giving us the power to prevent it. The responsibility thus given to humanity is enormous and asks to be balanced by reverence for new life as a moral feeling of soul.

Under the influence of Lucifer and Ahriman, the sexual act is in danger of becoming rather commonplace and risks no longer being recognized as the highest of creative human gifts. We can see this demonstrated in the sex scenes that seem to be mandatory in films, books and other forms of entertainment. Sex sells. It would appear that we have mistaken its creative spiritual force towards new birth as the ultimate in amusement, whereas in truth, it is mysterious and holy. Alongside this degradation is the tendency to deny the true value of the home, grading its upkeep as one of the less desirable vocations. It is as though the way we enter life on earth is being threatened.

The reality of our start in life is that it sows a seed for future rebirth that lies in more than just the sexual act. The power to reproduce works in all aspects of thoughts, feelings and motivation. It is expressed by the human will to act, to perform deeds, to work. It lives in our intentions and our ability to initiate. Every human deed brings about a new birth, be it in thought, in effect upon the world at large, or upon life itself. To produce something requires an act of will and will-power can create anything! Therefore, one should never underestimate the power of the will, because in so far as it can bring about new life, it can also be the cause of death. Will-power used for evil can, and does, kill. Nevertheless, usually in daily life at home, we come across negative will forces in less dangerous ways, such as in selfishness, laziness, greed, ambition, or other anti-social qualities.

Being a homemaker means that one knows only too well how important it is not to want in a selfish way. Children who want for want's sake, can become bottomless pits down which every effort to please falls. Most people have little time for the so-called spoilt child. But wanting for the sake of development, or intentionality that inspires deeds of love is another matter altogether. Wanting the good brings the good to birth. It is creativity at its best.

Children who fuss, or behave badly may be the result of having their wishes met too easily, but what we term wilful may come from other causes. It may be that the child's experience of the world and its own power of motivation do not match up. Children who have poor speech, or suffer from dyslexia may need more will-power than those who are more fortunate in their gifts. The temper tantrum can have more than one reason for appearing! Stimulating an active life with lots of things to do, as well as developing as many practical skills as can be taught, will help to direct motivation into more constructive lines. The frustration of poor communication can be overcome by knowing how to *do* things well, even if one cannot read or write very well.

Unfortunately, low self-esteem and self-confidence have

become common in the life of homemakers. Everything else in the world can seem more valuable and dynamic than life at home to those who do not know their own worth. The beginning of raising one's confidence and appreciation of the life that one has chosen to live, is to gain a mastery over its secrets. Only then can one perform the jobs that one's vocation demands. Once the mysteries, the intricacies and the skills have been acquired, one will have developed the self-confidence to stand for the consequences of one's actions. Daily life and the future that it brings are now within one's grasp. Using initiative becomes an enjoyable activity. One will no longer hesitate but will be able to follow up one's intentions and achieve what one has set out to do, perhaps not always, but certainly more often. Self-confidence based on real understanding of the task can overcome almost all obstacles, and transforms hard grind into exciting new potential.

The power of reproducing is very strong in us. We are generously motivated in our wish to see our deeds and their outcome live on into the future. We rarely do something only for the here and now, but usually hope that it will be of lasting value. Perhaps this universal human striving lies at the root of the frustration homemakers sometimes feel when faced with the same job over and over again. We want things to *stay* nice, clean and beautiful, and feel disappointed when we have to repeat the same chores every day. Fortunately, we also recognize, in the best of moments, that nothing really lives if it is merely a repetition. The home that is alive and lived in is a place penetrated by things done well and cheerfully. If pleasure and joy have been generated within its doors, then the work that inevitably follows will be worthwhile.

Achieving skills, acting on intentions, initiating new possibilities, and acquiring knowledge are the basis for being able to do anything in the world. It takes the whole of life to become wise, and along the way, we hope to bring about much that is good. It may take the birth of a baby to ensure the future of the human race, but it takes the performance of real deeds of love to ensure the future of society as an expression of human evolution. Without taking initiative, nothing new can enter, and what we see as potential in the members of the house-community depends on encouraging their good intentions.

Initiative and the Individual

Generally speaking, most people live with other people, perhaps not directly because each occupies their own home, but usually there is a neighbour fairly close by. People also work together, most jobs requiring more than one person to carry them out efficiently. Moreover, the general trend is to be on friendly terms with one's neighbours and work mates. It is human to care for each other and to be there for other people, especially in times of need. Neighbourliness used to be a very important part of the village or town, big cities even boasting of close-knit neighbourhoods. Some of the most community minded areas were the tenement blocks, ugly in their design but warm and human in the relationship that the inhabitants shared. Encouragement and support lay at the core of these groups of homes.

City life and country life today create a very different background of concern. The tendency in the city is to feel that one can be a free individual, not tied to other people's opinions and free to go one's own way in life. However, this type of freedom carries a rider in that one can be very lonely in a city full of people whom one does not really know. Country life offers a different social experience. Everybody tends to know everybody and everything there is to know about everybody. One can feel decidedly less free in self-expression and individuality if one's family history is everybody's business! But in such a setting we know very clearly who our friends are and on whom we can rely.

We are all shaped by our environment. We grow up in homes and neighbourhoods that lay the foundation of our social experience and aims. So where can one find the freedom to be an individual with one's own unique purpose for living as well as maintain and develop a socially warm environment?

To find freedom, we need to go in search of our own destiny. We need to discover our own particular path, our own special role in life and our own unique spiritual meaning of existence. Life can no longer be mapped out safely for us by family customs and family professions. People used to live with the security of knowing that they were destined to follow in their father's or mother's footsteps. But that certainty has long vanished into the cosy past. The human being of today faces exciting new possibilities. People used to ask of their destiny: *What will become of me?* But the modern young person now asks: *What will I become?*

Freedom to choose has given us the potential to use our initiative. However, it takes great courage to break with tradition and it takes sensitive observation to know which profession suits one's capabilities and inclinations. The world has truly become our playing field. But one can feel very, very lonely and exposed when one first steps out of the home, with the wide world at one's feet. And it can take considerable time to find that special group of friends with whom one feels connected, or a partner with whom one can create one's own home.

Encouraging initiative and the search for individual freedom is the task of the homemaker. However, encouraging a social sense is an equally important aspect. Coming from a social and forward looking home can give untold support to young people. The conviction that early independence strengthens children is a mistaken one. It certainly hardens them, but tends to render them less able for social living. They need to learn how to manage their own lives and it is so much better to do this in a known environment. Enough mistakes will be made once they have left home. However, in an environment based on the social art, one can find one's individual personality quite successfully whilst still at home. It is better to leave home when strong in one's self-image—even if real self-knowledge and self-confidence come later when one establishes one's own home—than to leave because one feels pushed out by peer pressure or a feeling of being no longer welcome at home.

Losing a member of the house-community arouses conflicting emotions. One feels sad, excited, happy to see them go with confidence, concerned about their ability to manage, confident in their good intentions and hopeful that one has invested them with enough courage to use their own initiative and good will wherever they go. And most of all, remembering one's own first foray into independent living, one wishes them the friendship of like-minded companions. If one has been the homemaker one set out to be, they will definitely come home for visits and from being parent, childminder or guardian, one turns into friend and social companion.

The Family

Most homes are built on family ties. The people living together belong to one family and share the same blood-line. Because of this close connection, some aspects of karma will also be shared. By the nature of heredity, there will be common memories, and a shared code of conduct. Many things can remain unspoken because they are simply understood to be so by the members of the family. However, to a stranger entering such a close-knit home, many things may need to be explained. In the past, family members saw loyalty to the family connections as part of their inborn inheritance.

Such strong family ties are not so common any more. It is not unusual to find members of the family who no longer fit into the unspoken and unwritten laws. It is as though a stranger has been born into the web of the family. This can pose some interesting questions to homemakers who seek to practise the social art. The individual who does not always fit in can be a challenge, both positive and negative. Should one help them to conform, or should one stand back, leaving them unencumbered and thus free to find their role and place in the home?

Both these choices can work within a social home, if attention is paid as to who this stranger really is and what his or her destiny may be within the family setting. However, it is important to recognize and accept the oddness as a search for the self. What is less helpful is if the difference is denied, or adulated as something that makes the person unduly special. Individual destiny needs space, time and a loving attitude in order to unfold in a healthy way. Certainly, conformity to the social rules and customs can always be expected, but forcing someone to be like the others is usually not very helpful in the long run.

In olden times, such individuals may have become outcasts, eccentrics, disappointed spinsters, or frustrated human beings, bitter and disillusioned because their difference remained unacknowledged and unaccepted. With our modern consciousness, sinking into the family blood-line, doing as has always been done without questions asked, does not really suit any longer. Human beings of today seek their individuality in order to become more able to love the world and all that it contains. We want to love from choice, not from obligation.

Empowering others to become themselves is no easy task. But it is stimulating, rewarding and inspiring when one gets close to achieving it. Who knows what the outcome will be? The individual who finally emerges may be a genius. Or a loving friend. Or an ordinary person with strong social gifts. Or just someone who knows their own worth and that their value is not part of the old family line, but new and independent in its mission.

Empowering has a wonderful spin-off. One recognizes one's own worth in the mirror of the other's freedom gained! The bitter, frustrated housewife is transformed into a warm and loving homemaker by the members of the family, home, or society whose self-esteem and confidence have been raised. The family home, previously built on obligation, can become a new kind of community built on freedom and mutual respect.

Community

Unlike the family that finds its connections through the family tree, communities are designed to embrace human beings who are unrelated in any other way than through a common bond of purpose. Their karma or destiny has led them to join forces for one reason or another. The smallest of communities is a marriage, or partnership. From such arrangements of united destinies, our children are born. Other types of communities come together for a variety of reasons, perhaps to create new life styles, perhaps to co-operate over an agricultural undertaking, perhaps to create a school. Or to found a home for people with disabilities.

Communities are formed to open the door to a richer and better future. Living together with other people from free choice and with no other obligations than a shared vision, creates potential that can move mountains. Many things can be achieved by a group of people who aim for the same end, which an individual might find more difficult to carry out alone. However, by choosing to live together, one is obliged to take on board everyone's opinions, ideas, dispositions and motives. This is an essential part of community building. We can rarely make things happen just the way we *want* them, just *because* we want them. We put ourselves into the position of learning from each other. Everyone's potential is brought into activity within a community. By learning to accept each other as individuals working out of a common spiritual activity, but who show this joint awareness in very different ways, a new form of appreciation arises. The true uniqueness of each one is empowered to become creative.

Communities of people who seek to live together for the upholding of social forms are the foundation of social renewal. The communes of the middle of the twentieth century may have foundered on the rocks of greed, beliefs, dictatorship, brain-washing, and other negative expressions of human weakness, but the ideal of a society that *shares* the important things in life is gaining in validity. From groups that are willing to learn from the mistakes that have been made, a new consciousness can come to birth.

The Home as Community

The home of today can be an expression of community. The regard we generate by practising the social art of homemaking allows the members of the home to find their own karma, to feel free to fulfil their own individual destiny, and so recognize their own potential. Human beings who know their worth, not from pride, but with certainty and confidence in their unique spiritual heritage, will bring good about wherever they go in life. To help such a high ideal to come about in practice, each person's biography needs to be nurtured and respected. Then the preciousness of life itself, in all its tiny little details, as well as in the larger brush strokes, contributes to the success of the whole. The individual who feels *recognized* will be able to perform far better in life outside the home as well as in it, than the person whose individuality is swallowed up by the environment.

The home that is based on the family need not be excluded from becoming a community by choice. Recognition of the fact that we have chosen through our karma to be born into the family, that our individual destiny keeps us connected to each other and that this is what the blood tie really means, is no different in its community endeavour than a group of people choosing to live together without a family connection. The apparent difference is the timing of the choice itself. The one takes place before birth, the other takes place during life on earth. Perhaps the freedom we seek is more obvious in the second place and so we regard the home that is based on community as more socially modern than those built on the family.

However, there can be as much freedom within the family home as there can be in community when we realize that individuals who are born into the family are also free, unique and spiritually striving. That we have a common destiny does not prevent *choosing* our connection *consciously*. As soon as we see that we can be connected because we choose to acknowledge our tie to each other, empowerment has begun. We can no longer take anyone for granted. Each one becomes a member of the house-community that constitutes the home. Our children are born to us so that they can grow up and find their place in the world. They have never been our possession. We value the sense of freedom possible within a partnership, and many couples try to create the same as husband and wife. No one likes to live in each other's pockets, nor to be beholden in any binding or restrictive way. We desire freedom in our relationships. We want to live together because we *love* each other. With such an attitude, we can empower all family members.

Once homemakers start to enjoy the community aspect that freedom of the individual creates within the home, the social side of the task opens up. There is nothing more rewarding and interesting than the unfolding of human potential. So much can be achieved by those who know they are recognized and know that there is another person who believes in them. Believing in someone is neither blind faith, nor fond fancy. It is confirming them to themselves as valid and good in the structure of society. This could be said to be the spiritual task of the homemaker, and like all spiritual activities, it can be practised in all aspects of ordinary daily life.

Practising the Social Art

Before one can begin to practise the social art, one must discover it! And having made the discovery, one needs to find out how one can apply this new way of living. Previously one went about one's daily life firmly embedded in the rhythms and customs of one's family or country. One thought little and rarely about changing one's life or social habits. One paid even less conscious attention to the fact that people live in biographical rhythms because one did not need to seek for an individual standard of living as one does today. However, the modern person needs to learn a great deal about how to live in harmony with the spirit as well as the worldly, and by understanding how the soul develops by means of these important life rhythms, a new social awareness can be engendered.

We live in seven-year cycles of progress, and certain elements are uppermost in the different seven-year periods. In the first three years of life, we settle into *rhythms* that lie forever at the root of our disposition and influence the next four years as these rhythms continue to work. Now what comes to the fore is the need to learn from active participation in daily life. *Warmth* of enthusiasm is the key-note for these tender years and goodness is the ground of experience. In the light of these processes, the early childhood years unfold. From seven years until early adulthood is reached at twenty-one, the soul thrives on *beauty*, followed by *truth*. The years at school can be filled with the vast and wonderful gifts of nature and the universe that find meaning and relevance in the daily life of the growing young person. Intelligent thinking thrives now on what the world can offer from its store of treasures.

If these formative years have gone well, the adult period of twenty-one to thirty-five holds great and glorious discoveries! *Individual input* into daily life brings in one's daily bread and this develops into the *ability to see the meaning* one has in relation to other people's needs. If the earlier periods have been dry and unfruitful, then these two seven-year phases can be the beginning of lowering self-esteem as one finds that one has too little input into the world around one. Unemployment is one of the worst flatteners of confidence and enthusiasm.

At thirty-three, approximately, something new enters the biographical rhythm. Just as at three years of age, one first has a real sense of individuality, so at thirty-three, one has one's first real experience of the *consequences one single life* can have on the totality of the world. Now the choice has to be made, to follow one's inner destiny, or to become effective and rich in worldly terms. This is often the age when women start to feel their biological clock ticking. This is the age when men begin to make their mark in business.

From thirty-five to forty-nine, *managing* home, family, and a business efficiently and dynamically becomes one's target. Life has greater meaning the more one works and the harder one plays. One has little time for sentimentality but all the time in the world for intelligent far-sightedness. Then follow softer years. After fifty, one recognizes that one can no longer rule every particle of daily life and that the unexpected can still bring life in its wake. For women this can be a new lease of life. For men it can be a time of uncertainty as to how they can manage their old age adequately. If the previous periods have been too rigidly structured, then the seven-year phase in the fifties, which should be a time of developing inner resources, can be a time of suffering, But if the last years of the forties have been given up to delegating responsibilities, this period of the fifties can be a *time of learning*. Retirement comes at around the middle-sixties and now one can let younger folk battle for mastery of the world, enjoying the relaxation of the *beginning of wisdom*. On reaching seventy, one can begin to enjoy the *unfolding of an inner life* made all the richer by the full involvement one had in worldly things.

No matter where we are in our path of life, our guardian angel is always present. We know that in the early seven-year periods, help and protection is offered unstintingly. Moral forces are developed in us with their guidance. Later on, once adulthood is reached, especially after twenty-eight years approximately, we realize that help will be given only when asked. The morality that we have learned from our parents and the inner voice of conscience that our guardian angel awakens in us should become a bright star. Whenever we turn towards this inner light, answers are born. However, they no longer arrive of their own accord. We have to approach the angels out of our own free will.

Lucifer, however, has not given up his efforts to interfere and so he has succeeded in damaging the harmony of our seven-year rhythms. His first success at corruption happens when puberty arrives. Here we are, fully physically mature and able to produce offspring, but clearly spiritually quite unready and usually quite unprepared. Bringing up one's children when still a child is not uncommon in many parts of the world, but the extended family is still in full working order and so it is often the grandmother, who may be in her thirties, who is actually responsible for their education.

The second time that Lucifer's blinding influence spreads over us is when we begin to create a home. If we start in our twenties, our real social conscience is not yet fully ripened. We feel that we should be out there, finding out that our lives make a difference, but instead we are inside, trying to practise the social art, which we have usually not yet fully recognized. We are trying to focus on educating children, often without realizing that we can ask for the help of the guardian angels, not only our own, but those belonging to every single person in the home.

However, homemakers who observe the patterns that the biographical rhythms create in human beings can work much more generously and caringly with the house-community, no matter what their own age, or the age of its members. The variety of attitudes uppermost in the different life phases mirror the seven attitudes that make up the social art. Blending their qualities harmoniously, or enjoying the predominance of one or the other adds sparkle and dynamic to life in the home. Sometimes, simply by recognizing where someone is at in a particular seven-year period, can be very helpful when trying to understand a problem, or the onset of soul pain, or a serious illness that occurs. It is a major part of practising the social art.

The social art revitalizes many areas of ordinary life. Finding the meaning of the rhythms that appear in life is a good basis for healthy living. There is absolutely no doubt that sound relationships based on objective and warm regard for each other cannot fail to create a healthy society. Living with art, and allowing people to become creative in whatever way they have been gifted, adorns society and softens the hard contours of practical daily life. Being able to meet the needs of ordinary life, caring for each other and promoting this as a healthy attitude makes society less selfish and more human. Wanting to learn and to develop oneself so that the regard and respect each one has for the other can empower individuals to express their freedom responsibly, creates the potential for honesty and selflessness.

The seven processes of life link up the seven-year

biographical rhythms and connect with the seven attitudes of the social art. The house-community that is inspired by this knowledge is lively, creative, interesting and enjoyable. People who are allowed to grow up in homes that practise the social art can move out into society with positive, forward looking attitudes. They know what community is. They understand life. They know how to *do* things, how to look after themselves, but most of all, they know *how to look after others*. They have lived in a community of free souls who share life because they love each other, warts and all!

The Development of Humanity as a Social Being

Human beings were not always social in the way that we understand today. By observing the gradual change in social abilities of children, one can see how humanity has progressed. It is as though the social development that we can see in history repeats itself in the individual from birth right into adulthood. For example, babies seem to need no one, except for food. In fact, they need someone to love them unstintingly. As toddlers, children play side by side, or back to back, and only begin to play together after the age of approximately four years. Then they need to be taught to socialize, and learn it best in kindergartens or from siblings or other young children. From around seven years, children start to acquire social awareness learned from adults such as teachers or parents. Usually, by the time they have reached adolescence, growing individuals can socialize out of their own accord. Customs can be applied by choice, and a social conscience is born because of the gradual change in thinking, and therefore in awareness of other people's needs and rights.

From myths and legends of the far, far past, one can see how we have progressed from caring for our immediate blood relatives in order to be safe from attack, to justice that was crude and compelling, to 'an eye for an eye' approach to problems, to the law, and lately to civil rights and human rights. We can see that as our thinking changed, so too did our social habits. In the past we have been graced by spiritual leaders who incarnated and sacrificed in the service of humanity's search for individual freedom. These great leaders and examples of spiritual integrity have taught us that freedom and individuality can be dangerous weapons within the confines of a narrow-minded society. Without compassion and love they become power and might. We are on the road to learning this basic lesson but are still under the influence of Ahriman who brought humanity closer to material knowledge and gain with the age of discovery and the rise of science. We learnt so much about our bodies, our abilities and our potential as giants of the earth. We learnt to control matter because we learnt to understand how it works. However, in so doing, we almost forgot the other aspect of our true being, which is our spiritual heritage. Under Lucifer's misguidance, we began to imagine that our social life, too, could be legislated and that spiritual individuality would find enough freedom by itself, within the society that was formed.

With the rise of materialistic thinking and scientific knowledge, many religions, and occult societies that held great spiritual power, lost the understanding of their own heritage and became dogmatic traditions, or secret societies. And the very institutions that might have carried the inner spiritual guidance of humanity lost their incentive because no one believed in a spiritual foundation any more. For example, the Freemasons used to be the first to recognize new potential and saw trends in society that they cultivated for the good of humanity's development. Their very name implies building for freedom. In the Middle Ages, all the great craftsmen and artists belonged to this stream of spiritual activity, influencing the course of human evolution through the depth of their spiritual understanding of the world.

Today, each individual has to find his own path to knowledge. Occult groups are often only a road to greater earthly power. What was once revered as a search for wisdom, beauty and strength of spirit has sunk into science of the earth, art that keeps no secrets, and religions that enlightened individuals might be wise to ignore. We know we seek for liberty, equality, and fraternity but we may have lost a true direction towards their acquisition because we place them in an order that cannot be fulfilled without exercising selfishness. Because of the interference of Lucifer and Ahriman, the lessons of compassion and love that should have led humanity to greater freedom have been dimmed. Fear of other people's way of thinking and believing led to building walls between nations and peoples. Loneliness and selfishness grew.

The lonely home of today is very, very new. Before the First World War, homes were a stronghold of education, standards and values. Family traditions and professions were solid and established. The home was one's castle. Everyone's home was different but this was accepted as within one's rights. Different ways of belief, different standards of living were also accepted as normal. One did not expect every one to be or have the same. One did not, coming from the security of the *rightness* of one's upbringing, need to fight over it.

Something as profoundly destructive as nationalism, for which wars are now being fought, was a non-issue. One fought over land and territory, and later over principles. The Second World War went one step further and made racial hatred the reason for mass genocide. No society could remain unchanged or untouched by such inhuman deeds. Perhaps one could even imagine that something human and warm died in us. In its aftermath many values disintegrated, and amongst them the home as we used to know it also disappeared. The rebirth of a living social conscience lies at the core of the need to learn to see and practise the social art. The spiritual task that occult societies such as the Freemasons carried can no longer be expected from highly developed initiates. All human beings, because of their spiritual potential and earthly knowledge, are now responsible for everything that happens in the world. We have, materially and spiritually, created a global village and, as we have seen, in a village, everyone knows everything about everyone else!

A village, however, is small and to begin something new it is best to start small! The home, too, is a miniature representative of society and so it can become a centre of development. Here new values and attitudes can be decided upon and practised quietly and lovingly. The home that lives out of the practice of the social art, opens its doors so that others can come in and see how compassion and love can work in individuals who still seek the meaning of love of humanity. The new home is small enough to allow this striving to germinate, grow, and shine in the world through the deeds of each of its members.

Home as the Foundation of a New Society

Human destiny cannot be solved by looking only at the larger picture. We have to begin in subtle ways to turn the tide and create a society that can empower individuals selflessly. Practising the great dance of human evolution at home may seem insignificant at first, but the reality is that small steps forward change the world. A beginning may be to find a new way of working with the precepts of liberty, equality and fraternity. By allowing *freedom of thought*, encouraging *common social rights* and practising a *fraternal sharing of economic gain* within the home, individuals can set out on a road of new discovery. We can learn from this new endeavour that the spiritual aspects in life are real and sustaining when times are hard. Inner self-worth will become strong. We can learn that where the law is concerned justice can only prevail if we are all equal under its rule. And lastly, we can realize a deep social conscience when we share our gains according to need rather than according to wants and wishes.

Restructuring these three great human expressions of spiritual activity is the task of every human being who understands that the body is not all, but that human beings have a soul and spirit that also needs attention. Recreating the home as a place where cultured minds can meet in a social setting can build bridges between many diverse patterns of thinking. Recognizing the social art of homemaking is the new way to uniting souls, so that a society can be founded on tolerant understanding of differences that are part of the vast spectrum that makes up the human race. Homemakers are in the forefront of the new discovery that humanity *can* live together creatively.

From very early on in life we want to acquire the ability to achieve skills, to practise intentionality and to carry the responsibility of our actions. Little children play at this all day long and their play, which is imitation of adult activity, is actually *work*. Little children work hard at play, learning so many skills and experiencing so many consequences. Of course, if they are allowed to play, this affords them a great deal of pleasure. They *love doing* things and pleasure is the beginning of a love of life. School offers the opportunity to learn about the world, though it may be presented in a structured and challenging way. At home, this is enhanced by learning to do things properly and skilfully. School age children *enjoy* learning new things, as long as world weariness is prevented from setting the example! With every new ability, a little step further on the way to freedom is achieved. As adults, we know that if we can do something well, we have an inner glow of confidence that radiates out into our social setting. Self-confidence of our own validity enables us to *love the world*. We are often fearful of what we cannot do, or do not understand and this fear creates the tensions and misunderstandings that lead to conflict. The more we encourage children and young people to gain in ability and skill, the greater will be the adult joy of life.

Once we have grown up, we deepen confidence in ourselves as we develop the ability to manage our livelihood adequately. We lose self-confidence if we cannot find work, or earn our living. The dignity and self-esteem that work affords far outweighs the stresses of labour that we sometimes enjoy complaining about! In old age, work takes on a different quality. Now it is something we are supremely grateful for having been able to do. We are grateful to those whose job it is to care for us, and to support us. Homes that encompass all the age groups experience the value of the differing attitudes towards the gift of having the will and the interest to work.

Finding the grace and love that provides space for everyone to make his or her own contribution to the life of the home is the greatest challenge to the homemaker. It can appear to be so much easier just to get on with it and do it oneself, especially where little children are concerned! Moreover, the patience and tolerance required to allow older people to help in the house, when they may need a long time to achieve a small result, can stand in the way of efficiency and give one the impression that one should not put such a burden on them. However, homemakers who share out the responsibilities within the home, each according to the level that child, young person, partner, or elderly relative can enjoy and handle, share the social creation of the home. It is not only the homemaker who makes the home a lovely place in which to be. It is the contribution of all who live in it, and the freedom to volunteer, as well as the responsibilities handed out, that creates the small society of the home.

Homemakers who decide to practise the social art have set themselves a very inspiring yet hard path to walk. Cultivating joy, patience, empathy, interest, warmth, humour and tolerance may seem to be rather a tall order! However, if one sets out to do something new and adventurous, one needs exactly the same qualities. They can be cultivated within the soul of the artist, as long as one *wants* to achieve their sustaining strength, even if, at first glance, one may think that they are either not there, or too difficult to acquire.

The Inner Life of the Social Artist

To develop any art requires discipline. Artists work very hard, often repeating endlessly until they feel that what they wished to portray, or what they see as spiritual truths, are clearly and beautifully expressed. No art can simply be pulled out of one's sleeve except, perhaps, by the few artists who are born as genius. The discipline of being prepared to start, make mistakes, acknowledge and learn from them, and then to start again, is the lot of every aspiring artist. The inspiration may rise up from within as a true perception, but the practice of it has to live out in the world, and it is here that the imperfections lie.

To sustain so deep and profound a commitment needs support. Every art has its own inner discipline. The social artist will have to discover the way of keeping the fire of inspiration and spiritual truth alight, just as all artists have to do. Coupled with the desire for self-development is the absolute need to find something to which to refer in times of stress, and that upholds one's aims in times of diminished consciousness. There is a tendency to imagine that one only needs spiritual insight and strength when life is tough, but it is often even more essential when life is easy. When things are running smoothly one can lose sight of all one's highest intentions under the false impression that one may have achieved them. Good times and bad times come and go, but the need to practise the social art remains constant.

One way of finding inner substance is through meditation. From times far back in human evolution, great spiritual insights were attained by means of meditation, although the methods of practice were different in the individual streams of spiritual striving as well as in the various parts of the world. From this variety, one can see that meditation would appear to be adaptable according to the level of consciousness as well as the life style that is being followed. Therefore, people living in the world of today have to go in search of a way of meditating that suits their life, interests, needs and aspirations. Once found, however, the actual *doing* of the meditation that has been chosen is the real key. Meditating does not work well on a one-off basis. One has to settle down to daily effort. After some time, one will notice a change in consciousness, not necessarily because one has gained any new and startling knowledge, but rather because one can manage one's daily life with less irritation and greater awareness. By a steady and constant attempt at meditation, the unconscious and powerful motives that live within the soul will fall into gentler and more constructive patterns of thinking, feeling and willing. The sheer discipline of daily meditation hones the will, focuses thinking, and calms the feelings. Life will begin to take on a slower and more acceptable pace, though in practice none of the chores or responsibilities will be any different from before. One's attitude to them, however, will become more peaceful and more insightful. The qualities that one needs in order to be a homemaker in the service of the social art will start to make their presence felt.

Another road to follow in the search for inner strength of spirit is the way of prayer. Just as meditation sharpens the three soul forces, so does prayer open the heart and mind to human endeavour. The destiny of those with whom one builds the house-community can become clear and moving in the face of prayer. For prayer to become sustaining, asking the help of spiritual beings in the service of what *one knows to be spiritually true*, rather than what one *would like* things to be, washes the soul with compassion for the weakness that make us all so very human. Regular prayer can lead to a depth of understanding of other people that is incomparable. However, in contrast to meditation, praying only in times of need is not a waste of time, and can be very comforting and truly effective because it leads one right up to the door of the love that one is trying to live in ordinary daily life.

Love is the third path that one can take in the service of the social art. Love is neither an idea, nor a feeling. It is, in fact, a practical deed. Cooking a meal so that someone can live, is a deed of love. Caring for another person so that their fears and miseries need not overwhelm them, is a deed of love. Encouraging children to learn, grow and explore life, is a deed of love. Looking after an elderly person so that life can have quality as well as comfort, is a deed of love. Living together with other people, although their ideas may not be identical to one's own, is a deed of love. Caring for the environment, encouraging culture, opening one's doors to strangers, all these are deeds of love. The greatest of these very ordinary everyday things is to uphold and recognize the intrinsic worth of every human being whom one may meet. In the mirror of the single human soul, the whole of humanity can be seen and understood, and therefore loved. By acknowledging the miracle of human life on earth, an understanding of the spirit can grow. Love for creation in its smallest and greatest is not beyond the bounds of our reach, because it lives in the marvellous human will to do the good.

The remarkable thing about the dedication of artists to their work is that their devotion is entirely out of their own free will. Working with the social art is no less an act of freedom. Based on the inner certainty that the social organism of the home can be an image of what society could become in the future is a challenge that can be met with the courage of conviction. Knowing that one has taken the challenge freely moves homemaking from the bench in the back row to the privileged seat at the forefront of developments. A new morality that is founded on practical deeds of love for one's fellow human beings can begin to be an expression of spiritual activity that everyone can understand.

The Social Art of Homemaking

Is homemaking a vocation or a profession? To answer this question honestly, one would have to understand how artists approach their work. They look upon it as the professional outcome of their vocation. To practise one's art is a calling. The gift lies deep within the human soul and cannot be denied expression. Artists are compelled to offer their insights to the world at large, and far from keeping their art a secret they enjoy and even revel in the publicity that an exhibition, publication, play or concert arouses. They spend their whole lives shaping and polishing their gift to a higher and more transparent sheen. Such dedication is entirely professional, but at its root lies a vocational quality of soul.

The professional aspect of homemaking is not something new. Young girls used to be apprenticed to housewives in order to learn how to run a household and rear children. The professional nanny is a residue of this ancient calling. Another sideline that we still see as a profession today is the midwife. Home economics is yet another part of the profession. A well-trained housekeeper was highly thought of professionally within the middle classes, and considered by her employers to be worth her weight in gold!

There is a profound comparison to be drawn from the combination of vocation and profession with regard to the task of homemaking. The calling for community-living is there, deep in the soul, but practising community building calls for a professional approach. Learning about the social art, warming to the insights that it offers, observing the life processes in human beings and in the universe, and trying out new ways to express these awe-inspiring truths, creates a socially artistic home.

The modern homemaker binds all of these aspects into a coherent whole, seeing the vocational side of the task as the incentive, and practising its outer expression as a profession. Vocations arise and we know that they die only if they remain unrecognized, or are deliberately ignored. Professionalism relies on practice so that one need never fall into bad habits. It asks for research and commitment to the task in hand. These creative manifestations of human endeavour join forces in the social art.

Homemakers working out of the social art create a home together with other people. Co-creativity depends upon recognition of the role and contribution of everyone involved in the work at hand, and so sharing becomes a key word. Shared responsibility means that each member of the house-community knows what the others are doing and recognizes that it is because of everybody's involvement that the home is a warm and precious place in which to live. The attention and care of the homemaker, supporting and loving every effort and initiative, may nevertheless mean that some intervention is necessary at times. However, by learning to observe the uniqueness of everyone in the home, a helping hand can be offered without infringing on any good intentions.

The social artist who recognizes the true value of interdependence will experience that directions of purpose can *arise*, and thus superimposing them will gradually become unnecessary. The house-community can work from consensus, rather than counting a show of hands, or one person making lone decisions. Homemaking means to build a community of people who are learning to exercise free will in order to express love for the world through their deeds and aspirations. Duty loses its sting by loving what one is destined to do in life. With this, homemaking becomes a professional vocation. Neither Ahriman nor Lucifer can have control or influence over love. The greatest freedom in life is to love the ordinary daily things as they come and go.

Homemaking with the social art is the foundation of a free and creative way of living. The upkeep of the home as well as the care and maintenance of the physical necessities are obviously things that have to be done. However, seen in the light of the seven processes of life, the value of the task can begin to shine through, which is awakening to the feeling of empathy, acknowledging the spiritual origin of humanity, and striving to generate a climate in which each person can fulfil his or her true destiny.

Everything that life can offer happens at home. Home is like a small world, encompassing all human endeavour, emotions, dramas and hopes. The homemaker's task is making a space for people to enjoy the dance of life. The patterns of destiny that the steps of the dance reveal are always unique and ever changing. The music is the breath of life, the laughter its warmth, the costumes are colours of imagination, the flow and form are metamorphoses of its original design. The name of the dance is the social art.

To make a home that is filled with meaning and enjoyment is a very special task. To wonder at what life holds as secret, to be able to experience awe when the secrets are revealed, and to feel reverence for the miracle of human talents, as well as love for humanity's failings is the greatest gift. Life has few recipes to hand out to the inquiring, developing soul. However, life holds many great and wonderful questions for the seeker of the meaning of human destiny.

Bibliography

R. Steiner, *Karmic Relationships, Volume 1* (Rudolf Steiner Press, London 1972)

R. Steiner, *Karmic Relationships, Volume V1* (Rudolf Steiner Press, London 1971)

R. Steiner, *Theosophy,* (Anthroposophic Press, Hudson 1994)

R. Steiner, *The Cycle of the Year* (Anthroposophic Press, New York 1984)

R. Steiner, *Man and the World of the Stars* (Anthroposophic Press, New York 1982)

R. Steiner, *The Riddle of Humanity* (Rudolf Steiner Press, London 1990)

R. Steiner, *The Four Sacrifices of Christ* (Anthroposophic Press, New York 1981)

R. Steiner, *The Human Soul in Relation to World Evolution* (Anthroposophic Press, New York)

R. Steiner, *Inner Aspects of the Social Question* (Rudolf Steiner Press, London 1974)

R. Steiner, *The Study of Man* (Rudolf Steiner Press, London 1966)

R. Steiner, *Earthly Death and Cosmic Life* (Spiritual Research Edition: Garber Communications Inc. Blauveldt 1989)

R. Steiner, *Verses and Meditations* (Rudolf Steiner Press, London 1993)

R. Steiner, *Man as a Being of Sense and Perception* (Steiner Book Centre, Vancouver 1981)

R. Steiner, *The Planetary Spheres and their Influence* (Rudolf Steiner Press, London 1982)

R. Steiner, *Wonders of the World* (Rudolf Steiner Press, London 1983)

R. Steiner, *Man's Being, his Destiny and World Evolution* (Anthroposophic Press. New York 1984)

R. Steiner, *Occult History* (Rudolf Steiner Press, London 1982)

R. Steiner, *The Spiritual Foundation of Morality* (Anthroposophic Press, Hudson 1995)

R. Steiner, *The Etherisation of the Blood* (Rudolf Steiner Press, London 1971)

R. Steiner, *The Occult Significance of the Bhagavad Gita* (Anthroposophic Press, New York 1968)

R. Steiner, *Angels* (Rudolf Steiner Press, London 1996)

R. Steiner, *From Jesus to Christ* (Rudolf Steiner Press, Sussex 1991)

R. Steiner, *How to Know Higher Worlds* (Anthroposophic Press, London 1994)

R. Steiner, *Inner Impulses of Evolution* (Anthroposophic Press, New York 1984)

R. Steiner, *A Modern Art of Education* (Rudolf Steiner Press, London 1981)

R. Steiner, *Rosicrucian Wisdom* (Rudolf Steiner Press, London 2000)

R. Steiner, *Results of Spiritual Investigation* (Rudolf Steiner Publications, New York 1971)

R. Steiner, *The Principle of Spiritual Economy* (Rudolf Steiner Press, London 1986)

R. Steiner, *World History in the Light of Anthroposophy* (Rudolf Steiner Press, London 1977)

R. Steiner, *Towards Social Renewal* (Rudolf Steiner Press, London 1992)

F. W. Zeylmans van Emmichoven, *The Foundation Stone* (Rudolf Steiner Press, London 1963)

A. Bittleston, *Our Spiritual Companions* (Floris Books, Edinburgh 1980)

K. König, *The First Three Years of the Child* (Floris Books, Edinburgh 1998)

K. König, *A Living Physiology* (Camphill Books: TWT Publications 1999)

K. König, *In Need of Special Understanding* (Camphill Books: TWT Publications 1986)

K. König, *Eternal Childhood* (Camphill Books: TWT Publications 1994)

A.C. Harwood, *The Way of the Child* (Sophia Books: Rudolf Steiner Press, London 1997)

A.C. Harwood, *The Recovery of Man in Childhood* (Myrin Books 1989)

B. L. Urieli, *Kaspar Hauser Speaks for Himself* (Camphill Books: TWT Publications 1993)

M. Luxford, ed., *The Higher Senses and the Seven Life Processes* (Camphill Books: TWT Publications)

M. Glöckler, *A Guide to Child Health* (Floris Books, Edinburgh 1990)

R. Hauschka, *Nutrition* (Mercury Press, New York)

G. Childs, *Balancing your Temperament* (Sophia Books: Rudolf Steiner Press, London 1999)

J. Sleigh, *Crisis Points* (Floris Books, Edinburgh 1998)

B. Lievegoed, *Phases* (Rudolf Steiner Press, London 1997)

M. Schmidt-Brabant, *The Spiritual Task of the Homemaker* (Temple Lodge, London 1998)

V. van Duin, *The Art of Living* (Kate Roth Publications 1999)

D. Carey, J. Large, *Family, Festivals and Food* (Hawthorn Press, Stroud 1982)

W. von Eschenbach, *Parzival* (Penguin Paperback 1980)

George G. Ritchie, *Return from Tomorrow* (Fleming H. Revel Co. 1988)

B. J. Eadie, *Embraced by the Light* (Thorson: Harper Collins 1995)

R. A. Moody, *Life After Life* (Bantam Doubleday Dell 1976)

Dr Gilbert Childs with Sylvia Childs

THE JOURNEY CONTINUES...
Finding a New Relationship to Death

Coping with the death of a relative or friend is often the most trying and difficult challenge many of us have to deal with in life. Indeed, our culture generally treats the issue of death with fear and dread. But is it possible for this most mysterious fact of existence to be approached in another way? Gilbert Childs shows how we can find a new relationship to death by considering that the journey of life continues beyond the point at which we shed our physical body. Basing his position on the work of the scientist of the spirit Rudolf Steiner, he argues that human beings are only secondly beings of matter, and primarily spiritual beings.

Dr Childs gives an overview of the human being as made up of body, soul and spirit and discusses different states of supra-consciousness. He describes how healthy communication can be achieved between the living and the dead, and follows the passage of the individual soul in the life after death.

SOPHIA BOOKS
112pp; ISBN 1 85584 086 3; £7.95